William Randolph Hearst, Mary Hallock Foote, Noah Brooks

Stories by American Authors

William Randolph Hearst, Mary Hallock Foote, Noah Brooks

Stories by American Authors

ISBN/EAN: 9783744705219

Printed in Europe, USA, Canada, Australia, Japan

Cover: Foto ©Thomas Meinert / pixelio.de

More available books at **www.hansebooks.com**

Stories by
American Authors

IV

Stories by American Authors.

IV.

Stories by
American Authors
IV.

NEW YORK
CHARLES SCRIBNER'S SONS
1891

MISS GRIEF.

By Constance Fenimore Woolson.

"A CONCEITED FOOL" is a not uncommon
expression. Now, I know that I am not a
fool, but I also know that I am conceited. But,
candidly, can it be helped if one happens to be
young, well and strong, passably good-looking,
with some money that one has inherited and more
that one has earned—in all, enough to make life
comfortable—and if upon this foundation rests also
the pleasant superstructure of a literary success?
The success is deserved, I think : certainly it was
not lightly gained. Yet even with this I fully appreciate its rarity. Thus, I find myself very well
entertained in life : I have all I wish in the way of
society, and a deep, though of course carefully
concealed, satisfaction in my own little fame ;
which fame I foster by a gentle system of non-in-
terference. I know that I am spoken of as "that

quiet young fellow who writes those delightful little studies of society, you know ;'' and I live up to that definition.

A year ago I was in Rome, and enjoying life particularly. I had a large number of my acquaintances there, both American and English, and no day passed without its invitation. Of course I understood it : it is seldom that you find a literary man who is good-tempered, well-dressed, sufficiently provided with money, and amiably obedient to all the rules and requirements of ''society.'' ''When found, make a note of it ;'' and the note was generally an invitation.

One evening, upon returning to my lodgings, my man Simpson informed me that a person had called in the afternoon, and upon learning that I was absent had left not a card, but her name—'' Miss Grief.'' The title lingered—Miss Grief ! '' Grief has not so far visited me here,'' I said to myself, dismissing Simpson and seeking my little balcony for a final smoke, '' and she shall not now. I shall take care to be 'not at home' to her if she continues to call.'' And then I fell to thinking of Isabel Abercrombie, in whose society I had spent that and many evenings : they were golden thoughts.

The next day there was an excursion ; it was late when I reached my rooms, and again Simpson informed me that Miss Grief had called.

'' Is she coming continuously ?'' I said, half to myself.

" Yes, sir : she mentioned that she should call again."

" How does she look ?"

" Well, sir, a lady, but not so prosperous as she was, I should say," answered Simpson, discreetly.

" Young ?"

" No, sir."

" Alone ?"

" A maid with her, sir."

But once outside in my little high-up balcony with my cigar, I again forgot Miss Grief and whatever she might represent. Who would not forget in that moonlight, with Isabel Abercrombie's face to remember ?

The stranger came a third time, and I was absent ; then she let two days pass, and began again. It grew to be a regular dialogue between Simpson and myself when I came in at night : " Grief to-day ?"

" Yes, sir."

" What time ?"

" Four, sir."

" Happy the man," I thought, " who can keep her confined to a particular hour !"

But I should not have treated my visitor so cavalierly if I had not felt sure that she was eccentric and unconventional—qualities extremely tiresome in a woman no longer young or attractive. If she were not eccentric she would not have persisted in coming to my door day after day in this silent way, without stating her errand, leaving a note, or presenting her credentials in any shape. I made up my mind that she had something to sell—a bit of carving or some intaglio supposed to be antique. It was known that I had a fancy for oddities. I said to myself, "She has read or heard of my 'Old Gold' story, or else 'The Buried God,' and she thinks me an idealizing ignoramus upon whom she can impose. Her sepulchral name is at least not Italian ; probably she is a sharp country-woman of mine, turning, by means of the present æsthetic craze, an honest penny when she can."

She had called seven times during a period of two weeks without seeing me, when one day I happened to be at home in the afternoon, owing to a pouring rain and a fit of doubt concerning Miss Abercrombie. For I had constructed a careful theory of that young lady's characteristics in my own mind, and she had lived up to it delightfully until the previous evening, when with one word she had blown it to atoms and taken flight, leaving me standing, as it were, on a desolate shore, with nothing but a handful of mistaken inductions wherewith to console myself. I do not know a more exasperating frame of mind, at least for a constructor of theories. I could not write, and so I took up a French novel (I model myself a little on Balzac). . I had been turning over its pages but a few moments when Simpson knocked, and, entering softly, said, with just a shadow of a smile on his well-trained face, "Miss Grief." I briefly consigned Miss Grief to all the Furies, and then, as he still lingered—perhaps not knowing where they resided—I asked where the visitor was.

"Outside, sir—in the hall. I told her I would see if you were at home."

"She must be unpleasantly wet if she had no carriage."

"No carriage, sir : they always come on foot. I think she *is* a little damp, sir."

"Well, let her in ; but I don't want the maid. I may as well see her now, I suppose, and end the affair."

"Yes, sir."

I did not put down my book. My visitor should have a hearing, but not much more : she had sacrificed her womanly claims by her persistent attacks upon my door. Presently Simpson ushered her in. "Miss Grief," he said, and then went out, closing the curtain behind him.

A woman—yes, a lady—but shabby, unattractive, and more than middle-aged.

I rose, bowed slightly, and then dropped into my chair again, still keeping the book in my hand. "Miss Grief ?" I said interrogatively as I indicated a seat with my eyebrows.

"Not Grief," she answewed—"Crief : my name is Crief."

She sat down, and I saw that she held a small flat box.

"Not carving, then," I thought—"probably old lace, something that belonged to Tullia or Lucrezia Borgia." But as she did not speak I found myself obliged to begin : " You have been here, I think, once or twice before ?"

" Seven times ; this is the eighth."

A silence.

· " I am often out ; indeed, I may say that I am never in," I remarked carelessly.

" Yes ; you have many friends."

"—Who will perhaps buy old lace," I mentally added. But this time I too remained silent ; why should I trouble myself to draw her out ? She had sought me ; let her advance her idea, whatever it was, now that entrance was gained.

But Miss Grief (I preferred to call her so) did not look as though she could advance anything ; her black gown, damp with rain, seemed to retreat fearfully to her thin self, while her thin self retreated as far as possible from me, from the chair, from everything. Her eyes were cast down ; an old-fashioned lace veil with a heavy border shaded her face. She looked at the floor, and I looked at her.

I grew a little impatient, but I made up my mind that I would continue silent and see how long a time she would consider necessary to give due effect to her little pantomime. Comedy ? Or was it tragedy ? I suppose full five minutes passed thus in our double silence ; and that is a long time when two persons are sitting opposite each other alone in a small still room.

At last my visitor, without raising her eyes, said slowly, " You are very happy, are you not, with youth, health, friends, riches, fame ?"

It was a singular beginning. Her voice was clear, low, and very sweet as she thus enumerated my advantages one by one in a list. I was attracted by it, but repelled by her words, which seemed to me flattery both dull and bold.

"Thanks," I said, "for your kindness, but I fear it is undeserved. I seldom discuss myself even when with my friends."

"I am your friend," replied Miss Grief. Then, after a moment, she added slowly, "I have read every word you have written."

I curled the edges of my book indifferently; I am not a fop, I hope, but—others have said the same.

"What is more, I know much of it by heart," continued my visitor. "Wait: I will show you;" and then, without pause, she began to repeat something of mine word for word, just as I had written it. On she went, and I—listened. I intended interrupting her after a moment, but I did not, because she was reciting so well, and also because I felt a desire gaining upon me to see what she would make of a certain conversation which I knew was coming — a conversation between two of my characters which was, to say the least, sphinx-like, and somewhat incandescent as well. What won me a little, too, was the fact that the scene she was reciting (it was hardly more than that, though called a story) was secretly my favorite among all the sketches from my pen which a gracious public has received with favor. I never

said so, but it was ; and I had always felt a wondering annoyance that the aforesaid public, while
kindly praising beyond their worth other attempts
of mine, had never noticed the higher purpose of
this little shaft, aimed not at the balconies and
lighted windows of society, but straight up toward
the distant stars. So she went on, and presently
reached the conversation : my two people began
to talk.   She had raised her eyes now, and was
looking at me soberly as she gave the words of the
woman, quiet, gentle, cold, and the replies of the
man, bitter, hot, and scathing.   Her very voice
changed, and took, though always sweetly, the
different tones required, while no point of meaning, however small, no breath of delicate emphasis
which I had meant, but which the dull types could
not give, escaped an appreciative and full, almost
overfull, recognition which startled me.   For she
had understood me—understood me almost better
than I had understood myself.   It seemed to me
that while I had labored to interpret, partially, a
psychological riddle, she, coming after, had comprehended its bearings better than I had, though
confining herself strictly to my own words and
emphasis.   The scene ended (and it ended rather
suddenly), she dropped her eyes, and moved her
hand nervously to and fro over the box she held ;
her gloves were old and shabby, her hands
small.

I was secretly much surprised by what I had
heard, but my ill-humor was deep-seated that day,

and I still felt sure, besides, that the box contained something which I was expected to buy.

"You recite remarkably well," I said carelessly, "and I am much flattered also by your appreciation of my attempt. But it is not, I presume, to that alone that I owe the pleasure of this visit?"

"Yes," she answered, still looking down, "it is, for if you had not written that scene I should not have sought you. Your other sketches are interiors—exquisitely painted and delicately finished, but of small scope. *This* is a sketch in a few bold, masterly lines—work of entirely different spirit and purpose."

I was nettled by her insight. "You have bestowed so much of your kind attention upon me that I feel your debtor," I said, conventionally. "It may be that there is something I can do for you—connected, possibly, with that little box?"

It was impertinent, but it was true; for she answered, "Yes."

I smiled, but her eyes were cast down and she did not see the smile.

"What I have to show you is a manuscript," she said after a pause which I did not break; "it is a drama. I thought that perhaps you would read it."

"An authoress! This is worse than old lace," I said to myself in dismay.—Then, aloud, "My opinion would be worth nothing, Miss Crief."

"Not in a business way, I know. But it might be — an assistance personally." Her voice had sunk to a whisper; outside, the rain was pouring steadily down. She was a very depressing object to me as she sat there with her box.

"I hardly think I have the time at present—" I began.

She had raised her eyes and was looking at me; then, when I paused, she rose and came suddenly toward my chair. "Yes, you will read it," she said with her hand on my arm—"you will read it. Look at this room; look at yourself; look at all you have. Then look at me, and have pity."

I had risen, for she held my arm, and her damp skirt was brushing my knees.

Her large dark eyes looked intently into mine as she went on; "I have no shame in asking. Why should I have? It is my last endeavor; but a calm and well-considered one. If you refuse I shall go away, knowing that Fate has willed it so. And I shall be content."

"She is mad," I thought. But she did not look so, and she had spoken quietly, even gently.— "Sit down," I said, moving away from her. I felt as if I had been magnetized; but it was only the nearness of her eyes to mine, and their intensity. I drew forward a chair, but she remained standing.

"I cannot," she said in the same sweet, gentle tone, "unless you promise."

"Very well, I promise; only sit down."

As I took her arm to lead her to the chair I perceived that she was trembling, but her face continued unmoved.

" You do not, of course, wish me to look at your manuscript now ?" I said, temporizing ; " it would be much better to leave it. Give me your address, and I will return it to you with my written opinion ; though, I repeat, the latter will be of no use to you. It is the opinion of an editor or publisher that you want."

" It shall be as you please. And I will go in a moment," said Miss Grief, pressing her palms together, as if trying to control the tremor that had seized her slight frame.

She looked so pallid that I thought of offering her a glass of wine ; then I remembered that if I did it might be a bait to bring her there again, and this I was desirous to prevent. She rose while the thought was passing through my mind. Her pasteboard box lay on the chair she had first occupied ; she took it, wrote an address on the cover, laid it down, and then, bowing with a little air of formality, drew her black shawl round her shoulders and turned toward the door.

I followed, after touching the bell. " You will hear from me by letter," I said.

Simpson opened the door, and I caught a glimpse of the maid, who was waiting in the anteroom. She was an old woman, shorter than her mistress, equally thin, and dressed like her in rusty black. As the door opened she turned toward it a pair of small, dim blue eyes with a look of furtive suspense. Simpson dropped the curtain, shutting me into the inner room ; he had no

intention of allowing me to accompany my visitor
further. But I had the curiosity to go to a bay-
window in an angle from whence I could command
the street-door, and presently I saw them issue
forth in the rain and walk away side by side, the
mistress, being the taller, holding the umbrella :
probably there was not much difference in rank
between persons so poor and forlorn as these.

It grew dark. I was invited out for the evening,
and I knew that if I should go I should meet Miss
Abercrombie. I said to myself that I would not go.
I got out my paper for writing, I made my preparations for a quiet evening at home with myself ;
but it was of no use. It all ended slavishly in my
going. At the last allowable moment I presented
myself, and—as a punishment for my vacillation.
I suppose—I never passed a more disagreeable
evening. I drove homeward in a murky temper ;
it was foggy without, and very foggy within.
What Isabel really was, now that she had broken
through my elaborately-built theories, I was not
able to decide. There was, to tell the truth, a
certain young Englishman— But that is apart
from this story.

I reached home, went up to my rooms, and had a
supper. It was to console myself ; I am obliged to
console myself scientifically once in a while. I was
walking up and down afterward, smoking and feeling somewhat better, when my eye fell upon the
pasteboard box. I took it up ; on the cover was
written an address which showed that my visitor

must have walked a long distance in order to see
me : " A. Crief."—" A Grief," I thought ; " and
so she is. I positively believe she has brought all
this trouble upon me : she has the evil eye." I
took out the manuscript and looked at it. It was
in the form of a little volume, and clearly written ;
on the cover was the word "Armor" in German
text, and, underneath, a pen-and-ink sketch of a
helmet, breastplate, and shield.

" Grief certainly needs armor," I said to myself,
sitting down by the table and turning over the
pages. " I may as well look over the thing now ; I
could not be in a worse mood." And then I began
to read.

Early the next morning Simpson took a note
from me to the given address, returning with the
following reply : " No ; I prefer to come to you ;
at four ; A. CRIEF." These words, with their three
semicolons, were written in pencil upon a piece of
coarse printing-paper, but the handwriting was as
clear and delicate as that of the manuscript in ink.

" What sort of a place was it, Simpson ?"

" Very poor, sir, but I did not go all the way
up. The elder person came down, sir, took the
note, and requested me to wait where I was."

" You had no chance, then, to make inquiries ?"
I said, knowing full well that he had emptied the
entire neighborhood of any information it might
possess concerning these two lodgers.

" Well, sir, you know how these foreigners will
talk, whether one wants to hear or not. But it

seems that these two persons have been there but a few weeks ; they live alone, and are uncommonly silent and reserved. The people round there call them something that signifies ' the Madames American, thin and dumb.' "

At four the " Madames American" arrived ; it was raining again, and they came on foot under their old umbrella. The maid waited in the ante-room, and Miss Grief was ushered into my bachelor's parlor. I had thought that I should meet her with great deference ; but she looked so forlorn that my deference changed to pity. It was the woman that impressed me then, more than the writer—the fragile, nerveless body more than the inspired mind. For it was inspired : I had sat up half the night over her drama, and had felt thrilled through and through more than once by its earnestness, passion, and power.

No one could have been more surprised than I was to find myself thus enthusiastic. I thought I had outgrown that sort of thing. And one would have supposed, too (I myself should have supposed so the day before), that the faults of the drama, which were many and prominent, would have chilled any liking I might have felt, I being a writer myself, and therefore critical ; for writers are as apt to make much of the " how," rather than the " what," as painters, who, it is well known, prefer an exquisitely rendered representation of a commonplace theme to an imperfectly executed picture of even the most striking subject.

But in this case, on the contrary, the scattered rays of splendor in Miss Grief's drama had made me forget the dark spots, which were numerous and disfiguring ; or, rather, the splendor had made me anxious to have the spots removed. And this also was a philanthropic state very unusual with me. Regarding unsuccessful writers, my motto had been '' Væ victis !''

My visitor took a seat and folded her hands ; I could see, in spite of her quiet manner, that she was in breathless suspense. It seemed so pitiful that she should be trembling there before me—a woman so much older than I was, a woman who possessed the divine spark of genius, which I was by no means sure (in spite of my success) had been granted to me—that I felt as if I ought to go down on my knees before her, and entreat her to take her proper place of supremacy at once. But there ! one does not go down on one's knees, combustively, as it were, before a woman over fifty, plain in feature, thin, dejected, and ill-dressed. I contented myself with taking her hands (in their miserable old gloves) in mine, while I said cordially, '' Miss Crief, your drama seems to me full of original power. It has roused my enthusiasm : I sat up half the night reading it.''

The hands I held shook, but something (perhaps a shame for having evaded the knees business) made me tighten my hold and bestow upon her also a reassuring smile. She looked at me for a moment, and then, suddenly and noiselessly, tears

rose and rolled down her cheeks. I dropped her
hands and retreated. I had not thought her tearful : on the contrary, her voice and face had
seemed rigidly controlled. But now here she was
bending herself over the side of the chair with her
head resting on her arms, not sobbing aloud, but
her whole frame shaken by the strength of her
emotion. I rushed for a glass of wine ; I pressed
her to take it. I did not quite know what to do,
but, putting myself in her place, I decided to
praise the drama ; and praise it I did. I do not
know when I have used so many adjectives. She
raised her head and began to wipe her eyes.

" Do take the wine," I said, interrupting myself
in my cataract of language.

" I dare not," she answered ; then added humbly, " that is, unless you have a biscuit here or a
bit of bread."

I found some biscuit ; she ate two, and then
slowly drank the wine, while I resumed my verbal
Niagara. Under its influence—and that of the
wine too, perhaps—she began to show new life.
It was not that she looked radiant—she could not
—but simply that she looked warm. I now perceived what had been the principal discomfort of
her appearance heretofore : it was that she had
looked all the time as if suffering from cold.

At last I could think of nothing more to say,
and stopped. I really admired the drama, but I
thought I had exerted myself sufficiently as an
anti-hysteric, and that adjectives enough, for the

present at least, had been administered. She had put down her empty wine-glass, and was resting her hands on the broad cushioned arms of her chair with, for a thin person, a sort of expanded content.

"You must pardon my tears," she said, smiling ; "it was the revulsion of feeling. My life was at a low ebb : if your sentence had been against me it would have been my end."

"Your end ?"

"Yes, the end of my life ; I should have destroyed myself."

"Then you would have been a weak as well as wicked woman," I said in a tone of disgust. I do hate sensationalism.

"Oh no, you know nothing about it. I should have destroyed only this poor worn tenement of clay. But I can well understand how *you* would look upon it. Regarding the desirableness of life the prince and the beggar may have different opinions.—We will say no more of it, but talk of the drama instead." As she spoke the word "drama" a triumphant brightness came into her eyes.

I took the manuscript from a drawer and sat down beside her. "I suppose you know that there are faults," I said, expecting ready acquiescence.

"I was not aware that there were any," was her gentle reply.

Here was a beginning ! After all my interest in her—and, I may say under the circumstances, my

kindness—she received me in this way ! However,
my belief in her genius was too sincere to be
altered by her whimsies ; so I persevered. "Let
us go over it together," I said. "Shall I read it
to you, or will you read it to me ?"

"I will not read it, but recite it."

"That will never do ; you will recite it so well
that we shall see only the good points, and what
we have to concern ourselves with now is the bad
ones."

"I will recite it," she repeated.

"Now, Miss Crief," I said bluntly, "for what
purpose did you come to me ? Certainly not
merely to recite : I am no stage-manager. In
plain English, was it not your idea that I might
help you in obtaining a publisher ?"

"Yes, yes," she answered, looking at me appre-
hensively, all her old manner returning.

I followed up my advantage, opened the little
paper volume and began. I first took the drama
line by line, and spoke of the faults of expression
and structure ; then I turned back and touched
upon two or three glaring impossibilities in the
plot. "Your absorbed interest in the motive of
the whole no doubt made you forget these blemishes," I said apologetically.

But, to my surprise, I found that she did not see
the blemishes—that she appreciated nothing I had
said, comprehended nothing. Such unaccountable
obtuseness puzzled me. I began again, going over
the whole with even greater minuteness and care.

I worked hard : the perspiration stood in beads
upon my forehead as I struggled with her—what
shall I call it—obstinacy ? But it was not exactly
obstinacy. She simply could not see the faults of
her own work, any more than a blind man can see
the smoke that dims a patch of blue sky. When I
had finished my task the second time she still remained as gently impassive as before. I leaned
back in my chair exhausted, and looked at her.

Even then she did not seem to comprehend
(whether she agreed with it or not) what I must be
thinking. "It is such a heaven to me that you
like it !" she murmured dreamily, breaking the
silence. Then, with more animation, "And *now*
you will let me recite it ?"

I was too weary to oppose her ; she threw aside
her shawl and bonnet, and, standing in the centre
of the room, began.

And she carried me along with her : all the
strong passages were doubly strong when spoken,
and the faults, which seemed nothing to her, were
made by her earnestness to seem nothing to me, at
least for that moment. When it was ended she
stood looking at me with a triumphant smile.

"Yes," I said, "I like it, and you see that I do.
But I like it because my taste is peculiar. To me
originality and force are everything—perhaps because I have them not to any marked degree myself—but the world at large will not overlook as I
do your absolutely barbarous shortcomings on
account of them. Will you trust me to go over

the drama and correct it at my pleasure ?'' This was a vast deal for me to offer ; I was surprised at myself.

" No,'' she answered softly, still smiling. " There shall not be so much as a comma altered.'' Then she sat down and fell into a reverie as though she were alone.

" Have you written anything else ?'' I said after a while, when I had become tired of the silence.

" Yes.''

" Can I see it ? Or is it *them ?*''

" It is *them.* Yes, you can see all.''

" I will call upon you for the purpose.''

" No, you must not,'' she said, coming back to the present nervously. " I prefer to come to you.''

At this moment Simpson entered to light the room, and busied himself rather longer than was necessary over the task. When he finally went out I saw that my visitor's manner had sunk into its former depression : the presence of the servant seemed to have chilled her.

" When did you say I might come ?'' I repeated, ignoring her refusal.

" I did not say it. It would be impossible.''

" Well, then, when will you come here ?'' There was, I fear, a trace of fatigue in my tone.

" At your good pleasure, sir,'' she answered humbly.

My chivalry was touched by this : after all, she was a woman. " Come to-morrow,'' I said. " By

the way, come and dine with me then ; why not ?"
I was curious to see what she would reply.

"Why not, indeed ? Yes, I will come. I am
forty-three : I might have been your mother."

This was not quite true, as I am over thirty : but
I look young, while she— Well, I had thought
her over fifty. " I can hardly call you ' mother,'
but we might compromise upon ' aunt,' " I said,
laughing. "Aunt what ?"

"My name is Aaronna," she gravely answered.
" My father was much disappointed that I was not
a boy, and gave me as nearly as possible the name
he had prepared—Aaron."

" Then come and dine with me to-morrow, and
bring with you the other manuscripts, Aaronna," I
said, amused at the quaint sound of the name. On
the whole, I did not like " aunt."

" I will come," she answered.

It was twilight and still raining, but she refused
all offers of escort or carriage, departing with her
maid, as she had come, under the brown umbrella.
The next day we had the dinner. Simpson was
astonished—and more than astonished, grieved—
when I told him that he was to dine with the maid ;
but he could not complain in words, since my own
guest, the mistress, was hardly more attractive.
When our preparations were complete I could not
help laughing : the two prim little tables, one in
the parlor and one in the anteroom, and Simpson
disapprovingly going back and forth between
them, were irresistible.

I greeted my guest hilariously when she arrived, and, fortunately, her manner was not quite so depressed as usual : I could never have accorded myself with a tearful mood. I had thought that perhaps she would make, for the occasion, some change in her attire ; I have never known a woman who had not some scrap of finery, however small, in reserve for that unexpected occasion of which she is ever dreaming. But no : Miss Grief wore the same black gown, unadorned and unaltered. I was glad that there was no rain that day, so that the skirt did not at least look so damp and rheumatic.

She ate quietly, almost furtively, yet with a good appetite, and she did not refuse the wine. Then, when the meal was over and Simpson had removed the dishes, I asked for the new manuscripts. She gave me an old green copybook filled with short poems, and a prose sketch by itself ; I lit a cigar and sat down at my desk to look them over.

" Perhaps you will try a cigarette ?" I suggested, more for amusement than anything else, for there was not a shade of Bohemianism about her ; her whole appearance was puritanical.

" I have not yet succeeded in learning to smoke."

" You have tried ?" I said, turning round.

" Yes : Serena and I tried, but we did not succeed."

" Serena is your maid ?"

" She lives with me."

I was seized with inward laughter, and began hastily to look over her manuscripts with my back toward her, so that she might not see it. A vision had risen before me of those two forlorn women, alone in their room with locked doors, patiently trying to acquire the smoker's art.

But my attention was soon absorbed by the papers before me. Such a fantastic collection of words, lines, and epithets I had never before seen, or even in dreams imagined. In truth, they were like the work of dreams : they were *Kubla Khan*, only more so. Here and there was radiance like the flash of a diamond, but each poem, almost each verse and line, was marred by some fault or lack which seemed wilful perversity, like the work of an evil sprite. It was like a case of jeweller's wares set before you, with each ring unfinished, each bracelet too large or too small for its purpose, each breastpin without its fastening, each necklace purposely broken. I turned the pages, marvelling. When about half an hour had passed, and I was leaning back for a moment to light another cigar, I glanced toward my visitor. She was behind me, in an easy-chair before my small fire, and she was —fast asleep ! In the relaxation of her unconsciousness I was struck anew by the poverty her appearance expressed ; her feet were visible, and I saw the miserable worn old shoes which hitherto she had kept concealed.

After looking at her for a moment I returned to my task and took up the prose story ; in prose she must be more reasonable. She was less fantastic perhaps, but hardly more reasonable. The story was that of a profligate and commonplace man forced by two of his friends, in order not to break the heart of a dying girl who loves him, to live up to a high imaginary ideal of himself which her pure but mistaken mind has formed. He has a handsome face and sweet voice, and repeats what they tell him. Her long, slow decline and happy death, and his own inward ennui and profound weariness of the rôle he has to play, made the vivid points of the story. So far, well enough, but here was the trouble : through the whole narrative moved another character, a physician of tender heart and exquisite mercy, who practised murder as a fine art, and was regarded (by the author) as a second Messiah ! This was monstrous. I read it through twice, and threw it down ; then, fatigued, I turned round and leaned back, waiting for her to wake. I could see her profile against the dark hue of the easy-chair.

Presently she seemed to feel my gaze, for she stirred, then opened her eyes. "I have been asleep," she said, rising hurriedly.

"No harm in that, Aaronna."

But she was deeply embarrassed and troubled, much more so than the occasion required ; so much so, indeed, that I turned the conversation back upon the manuscripts as a diversion. "I cannot stand that doctor of yours," I said, indicating the prose story ; "no one would. You must cut him out."

Her self-possession returned as if by magic.
"Certainly not," she answered haughtily.

"Oh, if you do not care— I had labored under
the impression that you were anxious these things
should find a purchaser."

"I am, I am," she said, her manner changing to
deep humility with wonderful rapidity. With such
alternations of feeling as this sweeping over her
like great waves, no wonder she was old before her
time.

"Then you must take out that doctor."

"I am willing, but do not know how," she
answered, pressing her hands together helplessly.
"In my mind he belongs to the story so closely
that he cannot be separated from it."

Here Simpson entered, bringing a note for me :
it was a line from Mrs. Abercrombie inviting me
for that evening—an unexpected gathering, and
therefore likely to be all the more agreeable. My
heart bounded in spite of me ; I forgot Miss Grief
and her manuscripts for the moment as completely
as though they had never existed. But, bodily,
being still in the same room with her, her speech
brought me back to the present.

"You have had good news ?" she said.

"Oh no, nothing especial—merely an invitation."

"But good news also," she repeated. "And
now, as for me, I must go."

Not supposing that she would stay much later in
any case, I had that morning ordered a carriage to

come for her at about that hour. I told her this. She made no reply beyond putting on her bonnet and shawl.

"You will hear from me soon," I said ; "I shall do all I can for you."

She had reached the door, but before opening it she stopped, turned and extended her _hand. "You are good," she said : "I give you thanks. Do not think me ungrateful or envious. It is only that you are young, and I am so—so old." Then she opened the door and passed through the ante-room without pause, her maid accompanying her and Simpson with gladness lighting the way. They were gone. I dressed hastily and went out —to continue my studies in psychology.

Time passed ; I was busy, amused and perhaps a little excited (sometimes psychology is excit-ing). But, though much occupied with my own affairs, I did not altogether neglect my self-imposed task regarding Miss Grief. I began by sending her prose story to a friend, the editor of a monthly magazine, with a letter making a strong plea for its admittance. It should have a chance first on its own merits. Then I forwarded the drama to a publisher, also an acquaintance, a man with a taste for phantasms and a soul above mere common popularity, as his own coffers knew to their cost. This done, I waited with conscience clear.

Four weeks passed. During this waiting period I heard nothing from Miss Grief. At last one morning came a letter from my editor. "The

story has force, but I cannot stand that doctor,"
he wrote. "Let her cut him out, and I might
print it." Just what I myself had said. The
package lay there on my table, travel-worn and
grimed ; a returned manuscript is, I think, the
most melancholy object on earth. I decided to
wait, before writing to Aaronna, until the second
letter was received. A week later it came.
"Armor" was declined. The publisher had
been "impressed" by the power displayed in
certain passages, but the "impossibilities of the
plot" rendered it "unavailable for publication"
—in fact, would "bury it in ridicule" if brought
before the public, a public "lamentably" fond of
amusement, "seeking it, undaunted, even in the
cannon's mouth." I doubt if he knew himself
what he meant. But one thing, at any rate, was
clear : "Armor" was declined.

Now, I am, as I have remarked before, a little
obstinate. I was determined that Miss Grief's
work should be received. I would alter and improve it myself, without letting her know : the
end justified the means. Surely the sieve of my
own good taste, whose mesh had been pronounced
so fine and delicate, would serve for two. I began ;
and utterly failed.

I set to work first upon "Armor." I amended,
altered, left out, put in, pieced, condensed,
lengthened ; I did my best, and all to no avail. I
could not succeed in completing anything that
satisfied me, or that approached, in truth, Miss

Grief's own work just as it stood. I suppose I went over that manuscript twenty times : I covered sheets of paper with my copies. But the obstinate drama refused to be corrected ; as it was it must stand or fall.

Wearied and annoyed, I threw it aside and took up the prose story : that would be easier. But, to my surprise, I found that that apparently gentle "doctor" would not out : he was so closely inter-woven with every part of the tale that to take him out was like taking out one especial figure in a carpet : that is, impossible, unless you unravel the whole. At last I did unravel the whole, and then the story was no longer good, or Aaronna's : it was weak, and mine. All this took time, for of course I had much to do in connection with my own life and tasks. But, though slowly and at my leisure, I really did try my best as regarded Miss Grief, and without success. I was forced at last to make up my mind that either my own powers were not equal to the task, or else that her perversities were as essential a part of her work as her inspirations, and not to be separated from it. Once during this period I showed two of the short poems to Isabel, withholding of course the writer's name. "They were written by a woman," I explained.

"Her mind must have been disordered, poor thing !" Isabel said in her gentle way when she returned them — "at least, judging by these. They are hopelessly mixed and vague."

Now, they were not vague so much as vast. But I knew that I could not make Isabel comprehend it, and (so complex a creature is man) I do not know that I wanted her to comprehend it. These were the only ones in the whole collection that I would have shown her, and I was rather glad that she did not like even these. Not that poor Aaronna's poems were evil : they were simply unrestrained, large, vast, like the skies or the wind. Isabel was bounded on all sides, like a violet in a garden-bed. And I liked her so.

One afternoon, about the time when I was beginning to see that I could not " improve" Miss Grief, I came upon the maid. I was driving, and she had stopped on the crossing to let the carriage pass. I recognized her at a glance (by her general forlornness), and called to the driver to stop : " How is Miss Grief ?" I said. " I have been intending to write to her for some time."

" And your note, when it comes," answered the old woman on the crosswalk fiercely, " she shall not see."

" What ?"

" I say she shall not see it. Your patronizing face shows that you have no good news, and you shall not rack and stab her any more on *this* earth, please God, while I have authority."

" Who has racked or stabbed her, Serena ?"

" Serena, indeed ! Rubbish ! I'm no Serena : I'm her aunt. And as to who has racked and stabbed her, I say you, *you*—you literary men !"

She had put her old head inside my carriage, and flung out these words at me in a shrill, menacing tone. " But she shall die in peace in spite of you," she continued. " Vampires ! you take her ideas and fatten on them, and leave her to starve. You know you do—*you* who have had her poor manuscripts these months and months !"

" Is she ill ?" I asked in real concern, gathering that much at least from the incoherent tirade.

" She is dying," answered the desolate old creature, her voice softening and her dim eyes filling with tears.

" Oh, I trust not. Perhaps something can be done. Can I help you in any way ?"

" In all ways if you would," she said, breaking down and beginning to sob weakly, with her head resting on the sill of the carriage-window. " Oh, what have we not been through together, we two ! Piece by piece I have sold all."

I am good-hearted enough, but I do not like to have old women weeping across my carriage-door. I suggested, therefore, that she should come inside and let me take her home. Her shabby old skirt was soon beside me, and, following her directions, the driver turned toward one of the most wretched quarters of the city, the abode of poverty, crowded and unclean. Here, in a large bare chamber up many flights of stairs, I found Miss Grief.

As I entered I was startled : I thought she was dead. There seemed no life present until she opened her eyes, and even then they rested upon

us vaguely, as though she did not know who we
were. But as I approached a light came into
them : she recognized me, and this sudden revi-
vification, this return of the soul to the almost
deserted bod, was the most wonderful thing I
ever saw. " You have good news of the drama ?"
she whispered as I bent over her : " tell me. I
know you have good news."

What was I to answer ? Pray, what would you
have answered, puritan ?

" Yes, I have good news, Aaronna," I said.
" The drama will appear." (And who knows ?
Perhaps it will in some other world.)

She smiled, and her now brilliant eyes did not
leave my face.

" He knows I'm your aunt : I told him," said
the old woman, coming to the bedside.

" Did you ?" whispered Miss Grief, still gazing
at me with a smile. " Then please, dear Aunt
Martha, give me something to eat."

Aunt Martha hurried across the room, and I followed her. " It's the first time she's asked for
food in weeks," she said in a husky tone.

She opened a cupboard-door vaguely, but I could
see nothing within. " What have you for her ?"
I asked with some impatience, though in a low
voice.

" Please God, nothing !" answered the poor old
woman, hiding her reply and her tears behind the
broad cupboard-door. " I was going out to get a
little something when I met you."

" Good Heavens ! is it money you need ? Here, take this and send ; or go yourself in the carriage waiting below."

She hurried out breathless, and I went back to the bedside, much disturbed by what I had seen and heard. But Miss Grief's eyes were full of life, and as I sat down beside her she whispered earnestly, " Tell me."

And I did tell her—a romance invented for the occasion. I venture to say that none of my published sketches could compare with it. As for the lie involved, it will stand among my few good deeds, I know, at the judgment-bar.

And she was satisfied. " I have never known what it was," she whispered, " to be fully happy until now." She closed her eyes, and when the lids fell I again thought that she had passed away. But no, there was still pulsation in her small, thin wrist. As she perceived my touch she smiled. " Yes, I am happy," she said again, though without audible sound.

The old aunt returned ; food was prepared, and she took some. I myself went out after wine that should be rich and pure. She rallied a little, but I did not leave her : her eyes dwelt upon me and compelled me to stay, or rather my conscience compelled me. It was a damp night, and I had a little fire made. The wine, fruit, flowers, and candles I had ordered made the bare place for the time being bright and fragrant. Aunt Martha dozed in her chair from sheer fatigue—she had watched many nights—but Miss Grief was awake, and I sat beside her.

"I make you my executor," she murmured, "as to the drama. But my other manuscripts place, when I am gone, under my head, and let them be buried with me. They are not many—those you have and these. See!"

I followed her gesture, and saw under her pillows the edges of two more copybooks like the one I had. "Do not look at them—my poor dead children!" she said tenderly. "Let them depart with me—unread, as I have been."

Later she whispered, "Did you wonder why I came to you? It was the contrast. You were young—strong—rich—praised—loved—successful : all that I was not. I wanted to look at you—and imagine how it would feel. You had success—but I had the greater power. Tell me, did I not have it?"

"Yes, Aaronna."

"It is all in the past now. But I am satisfied."

After another pause she said with a faint smile, "Do you remember when I fell asleep in your parlor? It was the good and rich food. It was so long since I had had food like that!"

I took her hand and held it, conscience-stricken, but now she hardly seemed to perceive my touch. "And the smoking?" she whispered. "Do you remember how you laughed? I saw it. But I had heard that smoking soothed—that one was no longer tired and hungry—with a cigar."

In little whispers of this sort, separated by long rests and pauses, the night passed. Once she asked if her aunt was asleep, and when I answered in the affirmative she said, "Help her to return home—to America : the drama will pay for it. I ought never to have brought her away."

I promised, and she resumed her bright-eyed silence.

I think she did not speak again. Toward morning the change came, and soon after sunrise, with her old aunt kneeling by her side, she passed away.

All was arranged as she had wished. Her manuscripts, covered with violets, formed her pillow. No one followed her to the grave save her aunt and myself ; I thought she would prefer it so. Her name was not "Crief," after all, but "Moncrief ;" I saw it written out by Aunt Martha for the coffin-plate, as follows : "Aaronna Moncrief, aged forty-three years, two months, and eight days."

I never knew more of her history than is written here. If there was more that I might have learned, it remained unlearned, for I did not ask.

And the drama ? I keep it here in this locked case. I could have had it published at my own expense ; but I think that now she knows its faults herself, perhaps, and would not like it.

I keep it ; and, once in a while, I read it over—not as a *memento mori* exactly, but rather as a memento of my own good fortune, for which I should continually give thanks. The want of one grain made all her work void, and that one grain was given to me. She, with the greater power, failed—I, with the less, succeeded. But no praise is due to me for that. When I die "Armor" is to be destroyed unread : not even Isabel is to see it. For women will misunderstand each other ; and, dear and precious to me as my sweet wife is, I could not bear that she or any one should cast so much as a thought of scorn upon the memory of the writer, upon my poor dead, "unavailable," unaccepted "Miss Grief."

LOVE IN OLD CLOATHES.

By H. C. Bunner.

Newe York, ye 1st Aprile, 1883.
Y^e worste of my ailment is this, y^t it groweth
not Less with much nursinge, but is like to those
fevres wch ye leeches Starve, 'tis saide, for that y^e
more Bloode there be in ye Sicke man's Bodie, y^e
more foode is there for ye Distemper to feede upon.
—And it is moste fittinge y^t I come backe to y^s my
Journall (wherein I have not writt a Lyne these
manye months) on ye 1st of Aprile, beinge in some
Sort myne owne foole and ye foole of Love, and a
poore Butt on whome his hearte hath play'd a
Sorry tricke.—
For it is surelie a strange happenninge, that I,
who am ofte accompted a man of ye Worlde, (as y^e
Phrase goes,) sholde be soe Overtaken & caste
downe lyke a Schoole-boy or a countrie Bumpkin,
by a meere Mayde, & sholde set to Groaninge and
Sighinge, &, for that She will not have me Sighe to

Her, to Groaninge and Sighinge on paper, wch is ye greter Foolishnesse in Me, y^t some one maye reade it Here-after, who hath taken his dose of ye same Physicke, and made no Wrye faces over it ; in wch case I doubte I shall be much laugh'd at.— Yet soe much am I a foole, and soe enamour'd of my Foolishnesse, y^t I have a sorte of Shamefull Joye in tellinge, even to my Journall, y^t I am mightie deepe in Love withe ye yonge Daughter of Mistresse Ffrench, and all maye knowe what an Angell is ye Daughter, since I have chose M^rs· French for my Mother in Lawe.—(Though she will have none of my choosinge.)—And I likewise take comforte in ye Fancie, y^t this poore Sheete, wh^on I write, may be made of ye Raggs of some lucklesse Lover, and maye ye more readilie drinke up my complaininge Inke.—

This muche I have learnt y^t Fraunce distilles not, nor ye Indies growe not, ye Remedie for my Aile.—For when I 1st became sensible of ye folly of my Suite, I tooke to drynkinge & smoakinge, thinkinge to cure my minde, but all I got was a head ache, for fellow to my Hearte ache.—A sorrie Payre !—I then made Shifte, for a while, withe a Bicycle, but breakinge of Bones mendes no breakinge of Heartes, and 60 myles a Daye bringes me no nearer to a Weddinge.—This beinge Lowe Sondaye, (wch my Hearte telleth me better than ye Allmanack,) I will goe to Churche ; wh. I maye chaunce to see her.—Laste weeke, her Eastre bonnett vastlie pleas'd me, beinge most cunninglie

devys'd in ye mode of oure Grandmothers, and
verie lyke to a coales Scuttle, of white satine.——

2nd Aprile.

I trust I make no more moane, than is just for a
man in my case, but there is small comforte in
lookinge at ye backe of a white Satine bonnett for
two Houres, and I maye saye as much.—Neither
any cheere in Her goinge out of ye Churche, &
Walkinge downe ye Avenue, with a Puppe by y^e
name of Williamson.

4th Aprile.

Because a man have a Hatt with a Brimme to it
like ye Poope-Decke of a Steam-Shippe, and
breeches lyke ye Case of an umbrella, and have
loste money on Hindoo, he is not therefore in y^e
beste Societie.—I made this observation, at y^e
Clubbe, laste nighte, in ye hearinge of W^mson, who
made a mightie Pretence, to reade ye Sp^t of y^e
Tymes.—I doubte it was scurvie of me, but it did
me muche goode.

7th Aprile.

Y^e manner of my meetinge with Her and fallinge
in Love with Her (for ye two were of one date) is
thus—I was made acquainte withe Her on a Wed-
nesdaie, at ye House of Mistresse Varick, ('twas a
Reception,) but did not hear Her Name, nor She
myne, by reason of ye noise, and of M^rsse Varick
having but lately a newe sett of Teethe, of wh. she
had not yet gott, as it were, ye just Pitche and
accordance.—I sayde to Her that ye Weather was

warm for that season of ye yeare.—She made answer She thought I was right, for Mr Williamson had saide ye same thinge to Her not a minute past —I tolde Her She muste not holde it originall or an Invention of W^{mson}, for ye Speache had beene manie yeares in my Familie.—Answer was made, She wolde be muche bounden to me if I wolde maintaine ye Rightes of my Familie, and lett all others from usinge of my propertie, when perceivinge Her to be of a livelie Witt, I went about to ingage her in converse, if onlie so I mighte looke into Her Eyes, wh. were of a coloure suche as I have never seene before, more like to a Pansie, or some such flower, than anything else I can compair with them.—Shortlie we grew most friendlie, so that She did aske me if I colde keepe a Secrett. —I answering I colde, She saide She was anhungred, having Shopp'd all ye forenoone since Breakfast.—She pray'd me to gett Her some Foode.— What, I ask'd.—She answer'd merrilie, a Beafesteake.—I tolde Her y^t that *Confection* was not on ye Side-Boarde ; but I presentlie brought Her such as there was, & She beinge behinde a Screane, I stoode in ye waie, so y^t none mighte see Her, & She did eate and drynke as followeth, to witt—

    iij cupps of Bouillon (wch is a Tea, or Tisane, of
        Beafe, made verie hott & thinne)
    iv Alberte biscuit
    ij éclairs
    i creame-cake

together with divers small cates & comfeits wh^{of} I
know not ye names.

So y^t I was grievously afeard for Her Digestion,
leste it be over-tax'd. Saide this to Her, however
addinge it was my Conceite, y^t by some Processe,
lyke Alchemie, wh^{by} ye baser metals are transmuted
into golde, so ye grosse mortall foode was on Her
lippes chang'd to ye fabled Nectar & Ambrosia of
ye Gods.—She tolde me 'twas a sillie Speache, yet
seam'd not ill-pleas'd withall.—She hath a verie
prettie Fashion, or Tricke, of smilinge, when She
hath made an end of speakinge, and layinge Her
finger upon Her nether Lippe, like as She wolde
bid it be stille. — After some more Talke, wh^{in}
She show'd that Her Witt was more deepe, and
Her minde more seriouslie inclin'd, than I had
Thoughte from our first Jestinge, She beinge call'd
to go thence, I did see Her mother, whose face I
knewe, & was made sensible, y^t I had given my
Hearte to ye daughter of a House wh. with myne
owne had longe been at grievous Feud, for ye folly
of oure Auncestres.—Havinge come to wh. heavie
momente in my Tale, I have no Patience to write
more to-nighte.

22nd Aprile.

I was mynded to write no more in y^s journall,
for verie Shame's sake, y^t I shoude so complayne,
lyke a Childe, whose toie is taken f^m him, butt
(mayhapp for it is nowe ye fulle Moone, & a moste
greavous period for them y^t are Love-strucke) I am

fayne, lyke ye Drunkarde who maye not abstayne
f^m his cupp, to set me anewe to recordinge of My
Dolorous mishapp.—When I sawe Her agayn, She
beinge aware of my name, & of ye division betwixt
oure Houses, wolde have none of me, butt I wolde
nott be putt Off, & made bolde to question Her,
why She sholde showe me suche exceed^s Coldness.
—She answer'd, 'twas wel knowne what Wronge
my Grandefather had done Her G.father.—I saide,
She confounded me with My G.father—we were
nott ye same Persone, he beinge muche my Elder,
& besydes Deade.—She w^d have it, 'twas no matter
for jestinge.—I tolde Her, I wolde be resolv'd,
what grete Wronge y^{is} was.—Y^s more for to make
Speache th^n for mine owne advertisem^t, for I knewe
wel ye whole Knaverie, wh. She rehears'd, Howe
my G.father had cheated Her G.father of Landes
upp ye River, with more, howe my G.father had
impounded ye Cattle of Hern.—I made answer,
'twas foolishnesse, in my mynde, for ye iii^d Generation to so quarrell over a Parsel of rascallie
Landes, y^t had long ago beene solde for Taxes, y^t
as to ye Cowes, I wolde make them goode, & th^r
Produce & Offspringe, if it tooke ye whole Wash^{tn}
Markett.—She however tolde me y^t ye Ffrenche
familie had.ye where w^{al} to buye what they lack'd
in Butter, Beafe & Milke, and likewise in *Veale*,
wh. laste I tooke much to Hearte, wh. She seeinge,
became more gracious &, on my pleadinge, accorded y^t I sholde have ye Privilege to speake with
Her when we next met.—Butt neyther then, nor

at anie other Tyme th^{after} wolde She suffer me to visitt Her. So I was harde putt to it to compass waies of gettinge to see Her at such Houses as She mighte be att, for Routs or Feasts, or ye lyke.—

But though I sawe Her manie tymes, oure converse was ever of y^{is} Complexⁿ, & ye accursed G.father sått downe, & rose upp with us.—Yet colde I see by Her aspecte, y^t I had in some sorte Her favoure, & y^t I mislyk'd Her not so gretelie as She w^d have me thinke.—So y^t one daie, ('twas in Januarie, & verie colde,) I, beinge moste distrackt, saide to Her, I had tho't 'twolde pleasure Her more, to be friends w. a man, who had a knave for a G.father, yⁿ with One who had no G.father att alle, lyke W^{mson} (ye Puppe).—She made answer, I was exceedinge fresshe, or some such matter. She clóath'd her thoughte in phrase more befittinge a Gentlewoman.—Att this I colde no longer contayne myself, but tolde Her roundlie, I lov'd Her, & 'twas my Love made me soe unmannerlie.—And w. y^{is} speache I att ye leaste made an End of my Uncertaintie, for She bade me speake w. Her no more.—I wolde be determin'd, whether I was Naught to Her.—She made Answer She colde not justlie say I was Naught, seeing y^t wh^{ever} She mighte bee, I was One too manie.—I saide, 'twas some Comforte, I had even a Place in Her thoughtes, were it onlie in Her disfavour.—She saide, my Solace was indeede grete, if it kept pace with ye measure of Her Disfavour, for, in plain Terms, She hated me, & on Her intreatinge of me to goe, I went.—Y^ls happ'd att ye house of M^rss Varicke, wh. I 1st met Her, who (M^rss Varicke) was for staying me, y^t I might eate some Ic'd Cream, butt of a Truth I was chill'd to my Taste all-readie.—Albeit I afterwards tooke to walkinge of ye Streets till near Midnight.—'Twas as I saide before in Januarie & exceedinge colde.

20th Maie.

How wearie is y^ls dulle procession of ye Yeare! For it irketh my Soule y^t eache Monthe shoude come so aptlie after ye Month afore, & Nature looke so Smug, as She had done some grete thinge. —Surelie if she make no Change, she hath work'd no Miracle, for we knowe wel, what we maye look for. —Y^e Vine under my Window hath broughte forth Purple Blossoms, as itt hath eache Springe these xii Yeares.—I wolde have had them Redd, or Blue, or I knowe not what Coloure, for I am sicke of likinge of Purple a Dozen Springes in Order.— And wh. moste galls me is y^ls, I knowe howe y^ls sadd Rounde will goe on, & Maie give Place to June, & she to July, & onlie my Hearte blossom not nor my Love growe no greener.

2nd June.

I and my Foolishnesse, we laye Awake last night till ye Sunrise gun, wh. was Shott att 4½ o'ck, & wh. beinge hearde in y^t stillnesse fm. an Incredible Distance, seem'd lyke as 'twere a Full Stopp, or Period putt to y^ls Wakinge-Dreminge, wh^at I did

turne a newe Leafe in my Counsells, and after
much Meditation, have commenc't a newe Chap-
ter, wh. I hope maye leade to a better Conclusion,
than them y^t came afore.—For I am nowe resolv'd,
& havinge begunn wil carry to an Ende, y^t if I
maie not over-come my Passion, I maye at ye least
over-com ye Melanchollie, & Spleene, borne y^{of}, &
beinge a Lover, be none ye lesse a Man.—To wh.
Ende I have come to y^{is} Resolution, to departe fm.
ye Towne, & to goe to ye Countrie-House of my
Frend, Will Winthrop, who has often intreated me,
& has instantlie urg'd, y^t I sholde make him a
Visitt.—And I take much Shame to myselfe, y^t I
have not given him y^{is} Satisfaction since he was
married, wh. is nowe ii Yeares.—A goode Fellowe,
& I minde me a grete Burden to his Frends when
he was in Love, in wh. Plight I mockt him, who
am nowe, I much feare me, mockt myselfe.

3rd June.

Pack'd my cloathes, beinge Sundaye.   Y^e better
ye Daie, ye better ye Deede.

4th June.

Goe downe to Babylon to-daye.

5th June.

Att Babylon, att ye Cottage of Will Winthrop,
wh. is no Cottage, but a grete House, Red, w.
Verandahs, & builded in ye Fash^n of Her Maiestie
Q. Anne.—Found a mightie Housefull of People.

—Will, his Wife, a verie proper fayre Ladie, who gave me moste gracious Reception, M^rss Smithe, ye ii Gresham girles (knowne as ye Titteringe Twins), Bob White, Virginia Kinge & her Moth^r, Clarence Winthrop, & ye whole Alexander Family.—A grete Gatheringe for so earlie in ye Summer.—In ye afternoone play'd Lawne-Tenniss.—Had for Partner one of ye Twinns, ag^st Clarence Winthrop & ye other Twinn, wh. by beinge Confus'd, I loste iii games.—Was voted a Duffer.—Clarence Winthrop moste unmannerlie merrie.—He call'd me ye Sad-Ey'd Romeo, & lykewise cut down ye Hammocke wh^ln I laye, allso tied up my Cloathes wh. we were att Bath.—He sayde, he Chaw'd them, a moste barbarous worde for a moste barbarous Use.—Wh. we were Boyes, & he did y^ls thinge, I was wont to trounce him Soundlie, but nowe had to contente Myselfe w. beatinge of him iii games of Billyardes in ye Evg., & w. daringe of him to putt on ye Gloves w. me, for Funne, wh. he mighte not doe, for I coude knocke him colde.

10th June.

Beinge gon to my Roome somewhatt earlie, for I found myselfe of a peevish humour, Clarence came to me, and pray^d a few minutes' Speache.—Sayde 'twas Love made him so Rude & Boysterous he was privilie betroth'd to his Cozen, Angelica Robertes, she whose Father lives at Islipp, & colde not containe Himselfe for Joye.—I sayinge, there was a Breache in ye Familie, he made

Answer, 'twas true, her Father & His, beinge
Cozens, did hate each other moste heartilie, butt
for him he cared not for that, & for Angelica, She
gave not a Continentall.—But, sayde I, Your
Consideration matters mightie Little, synce y^e
Governours will not heare to it.—He answered
'twas for that he came to me, I must be his allie,
for reason of our olde Friend^sp. With that I had
no Hearte to heare more, he made so Light of
suche a Division as parted me & my Happinesse,
but tolde him I was his Frend, wolde serve him
when he had Neede of me, & presentlie seeing my
Humour, he made excuse to goe, & left me to write
downe this, sicke in Mynde, and thinkinge ever of
ye Woman who wil not oute of my Thoughtes for
any change of Place, neither of employe.—For indeede I doe love Her moste heartilie, so y^t my
Wordes can not saye it, nor will y^is Booke containe
it.—So I wil even goe to Sleepe, y^t in my Dreames
perchaunce my Fancie maye do my Hearte better
Service.

12th June.

She is here.—What Spyte is y^is of Fate & y^e
alter'd gods! That I, who mighte nott gett to see
Her when to See was to Hope, muste nowe daylie
have Her in my Sighte, stucke lyke a fayre Apple
under olde Tantalus his Nose.—Goinge downe to
ye Hotell to-day, for to gett me some Tobackoe,
was made aware y^t ye Ffrench familie had hyred
one of ye Cottages round-abouts.—'Tis a goodlie

Dwellinge Without—Woude I coude speake with as much Assurance of ye Innsyde !

13th June.

Goinge downe to ye Hotell againe To-day, for more Tobackoe, sawe ye accursed name of W^{mson} on ye Registre.—Went about to a neighbouringe Farm & satt me downe behynd ye Barne, for a ½ an Houre.—Frighted ye Horned Cattle w. talkinge to My Selfe.

15th June.

I wil make an Ende to y^{is} Businesse.—Wil make no longer Staye here.—Sawe Her to-day, driven Home fm. ye Beache, about 4½ of ye After-noone, by W^{mson}, in his Dogge-Carte, wh. ye Cadde has broughten here.—Wil betake me to ye Boundlesse Weste—Not y^t I care aught for ye Boundlesse Weste, butt y^t I shal doe wel if haplie I leave my Memourie am^g ye Apaches & bringe Home my Scalpe.

16th June.

To Fyre Islande, in Winthrop's Yacht — ye Twinnes w. us, so Titteringe & Choppinge Laughter, y^t 'twas worse y^n a Flocke of Sandpipers.— Found a grete Concourse of people there, Her amonge them, in a Suite of blue, y^t became Her bravelie.—She swimms lyke to a Fishe, butt everie Stroke of Her white Arms (of a lovelie Roundnesse) clefte, as 't were, my Hearte, rather

yⁿ yᵉ Water.—She bow'd to me, on goinge into yᵒ
Water, w. muche Dignitie, & agayn on Cominge
out, but yˡˢ Tyme w. lesse Dignitie, by reason of
yᵉ Water in Her Cloathes, & Her Haire in Her
Eyes.—

17ᵗʰ June.

Was for goinge awaie To-morrowe, butt Clarence
cominge againe to my Chamber, & mightilie pur-
swadinge of me, I feare I am comitted to a verie
sillie Undertakinge.—For I am promis'd to Help
him, secretlie to wedd his Cozen.—He wolde take
no Deniall, wolde have it, his Brother car'd
Naughte, 'twas but yᵉ Fighte of theyre Fathers,
he was bounde it sholde be done, & 'twere best I
stoode his Witnesse, who was wel lyked of bothe
yᵉ Braunches of yᵉ Family.—So 'twas agree'd, yᵗ I
shal stay Home to-morrowe fm. yᵉ Expedition to
Fyre Islande, feigning a Head-Ache, (wh. indeede
I meante to do, in any Happ, for I cannot see Her
againe,) & shall meet him at yᵉ little Churche on yᵉ
Southe Roade.—He to drive to Islipp to fetch
Angelica, lykewise her Witnesse, who sholde be
some One of yᵉ Girles, she hadd not yet made her
Choice.—I made yˡˢ Condition, it sholde not be
either of yᵉ Twinnes.—No, nor Bothe, for that
matter.—Inquiringe as to yᵉ Clergyman, he sayde
yᵉ Dominie was allreadie Squar'd.

NEWE YORK, Yᵉ BUCKINGHAM HOTELL,
19th June.

I am come to yᵉ laste Entrie I shall ever putt
downe in yˢ Booke, and needes must yᵗ I putt it
downe quicklie, for all hath Happ'd in so short a
Space, yᵗ my Heade whirles w. thynkinge of it.
Yᵉ after-noone of Yesterdaye, I set about Counter-
feittinge of a Head-Ache, & so wel did I compasse
it, yᵗ I verilie thinke one of yᵉ Twinnes was mynded
to Stay Home & nurse me.—All havinge gone off,
& Clarence on his waye to Islipp, I sett forth for yᵉ
Churche, where arriv'd I founde it emptie, w. yᵉ
Door open.—Went in & writh'd on yᵉ hard Benches
a ¼ of an Houre, when, hearinge a Sounde, I
look'd up & saw standinge in yᵉ Door-waye,
Katherine Ffrench.—She seem'd muche astonished,
saying You Here ! or yᵉ lyke.—I made Answer &
sayde yᵗ though my Familie were greate Sinners,
yet had they never been Excommunicate by yᵉ
Churche.—She sayde, they colde not Putt Out
what never was In.—While I was bethynkinge me
wh. I mighte answer to yˡˢ, she went on, sayinge I
must excuse Her, She wolde goe upp in yᵉ Organ-
Lofte.—I enquiring what for ? She sayde to practice on yᵉ Organ.—She turn'd verie Redd, of a
warm Coloure, as She sayde this.—I ask'd Do you
come hither often ? She replyinge Yes, I enquir'd
how yᵉ Organ lyked Her.—She sayde Right well,
when I made question more curiously (for She grew
more Redd eache moment) how was yᵉ Action ? yᵉ
Tone ? how manie Stopps ? Whᵃᵗ She growinge

gretelie Confus'd, I led Her into ye Churche, & show'd Her y^t there was no Organ, ye Choire beinge indeede a Band, of i Tuninge-Forke, i Kitt, & i Horse-Fiddle.—At this She fell to Smilinge & Blushinge att one Tyme.—She perceiv'd our Errandes were ye Same, & crav'd Pardon for Her Fibb.—I tolde Her, If She came Thither to be Witness at her Frend's Weddinge, 'twas no greate Fibb, 'twolde indeede be Practice for Her.—This havinge a rude Sound, I added I thankt ye Starrs y^t had bro't us Together. She sayde if ye Starrs appoint'd us to meete no oftener y^n this Couple shoude be Wedded, She was wel content. This cominge on me lyke a last Buffett of Fate, that She shoude so despitefully intreate me, I was suddenlie Seized with so Sorrie a Humour, & withal so angrie, y^t I colde scarce Containe myselfe, but went & Sat downe neare ye Doore, lookinge out till Clarence shd. come w. his Bride.—Looking over my Sholder, I sawe y^t She wente fm. Windowe to Windowe within, Pluckinge ye Blossoms fm. ye Vines, & settinge them in her Girdle.—She seem'd most tall and faire, & swete to look uponn, & itt Anger'd me ye More.—Meanwhiles, She discours'd pleasantlie, askinge me manie questions, to the wh. I gave but shorte and churlish answers. She ask'd Did I nott Knowe Angelica Roberts was Her best Frend? How longe had I knowne of ye Betrothal? Did I thinke 'twolde knitt ye House together, & Was it not Sad to see a Familie thus Divided?—I answer'd Her, I wd. not robb a Man

of ye precious Righte to Quarrell with his Relations.—And then, with meditatinge on ye goode
Lucke of Clarence, & my owne harde Case, I had
suche a sudden Rage of peevishnesse y^t I knewe
scarcelie what I did.—Soe when She ask'd me merrilie why I turn'd my Backe on Her, I made Reply
·I had turn'd my Backe on muche Follie.—Wh. was
no sooner oute of my Mouthe than I was mightilie
Sorrie for it, and turninge aboute, I perceiv'd She
was in Teares & weepinge bitterlie. Wh^{at} my
Hearte wolde holde no More, & I rose upp & tooke
Her in my arms & Kiss'd & Comforted Her, She
makinge no Denyal, but seeminge gretelie to
Neede such Solace, wh. I was not Loathe to give
Her.—Whiles we were at This, onlie She had gott
to Smilinge, & to sayinge of Things which even y^{is}
paper shal not knowe, came in ye Dominie, sayinge
He judg'd We were the Couple he came to Wed.—
With him ye Sexton & ye Sexton's Wife.—My swete
Kate, alle as rosey as Venus's Nape, was for Deny-
inge of y^{is}, butt I wolde not have it, & sayde Yes.—
She remonstrating w. me, privilie, I tolde Her She
must not make me Out a Liar, y^t to Deceave ye Man
of God were a greavous Sinn, y^t I had gott Her
nowe, & wd. not lett her Slipp from me, & did soe
Talke Her Downe, & w. suche Strengthe of joie, y^t
allmost before She knewe it, we Stoode upp, & were
Wed, w. a Ringe (tho' She Knewe it nott) wh. belong'd to My G.father. (Him y^t Cheated Her^n.)—
  Wh. was no sooner done, than in came Clarence
& Angelica, & were Wedded in theyre Turn.—The

Clergyman greatelie surprised, but more att ye Largenesse of his Fee.

This Businesse beinge Ended, we fled by ye Trayne of 4½ o'cke, to y^{ls} Place, where we wait till ye Bloode of all ye Ffrenches have Tyme to coole downe, for ye wise Mann who meeteth his Mother in Lawe ye 1st tyme, wil meete her when she is Milde.—

And so I close y^{ls} Journall, wh., tho' for ye moste Parte 'tis but a peevish Scrawle, hath one Page of Golde, wh^{on} I have writt ye laste strange Happ wh^{by} I have layd Williamson by ye Heeles & found me ye sweetest Wife y^t ever

*   *   *

stopp'd a man's Mouthe w. kisses for writinge of Her Prayses.

TWO BUCKETS IN A WELL.

By N. P. WILLIS.

" FIVE hundred dollars a year!" echoed Fanny
Bellairs, as the first silver gray of the twilight spread over her picture.

" And my art," modestly added the painter,
prying into his bright copy of the lips pronouncing
upon his destiny.

" And how much may that be, at the present rate
of patronage — one picture a year, painted for
love !"

" Fanny, how can you be so calculating !"

" By the bumps over my eyebrows, I suppose.
Why, my dear coz, we have another state of existence to look forward to — old man-age and old
woman-age ! What am I to do with five hundred
dollars a year, when my old frame wants gilding
—(to use one of your own similes)—I sha'n't always
be pretty Fanny Bellairs !"

₊₊ *From " People I Have Met " (now out of print).*

" But, good Heavens ! we shall grow old together !" exclaimed the painter, sitting down at
her feet, " and what will you care for other admiration, if your husband see you still beautiful, with
the eyes of memory and habit."

" Even if I were sure he would so look upon me,"
answered Miss Bellairs, more seriously, " I cannot
but dread an old age without great means of em-
bellishment.   Old people, except in poetry and in
very primitive society, are dishonored by wants
and cares.   And, indeed, before we are old—when
neither young nor old—we want horses and otto-
mans, kalydor and conservatories, books, pictures,
and silk curtains—all quite out of the range of
your little allowance, don't you see !"

" You do not love me, Fanny !"

" I do—and will marry you, Philip—as I, long
ago, with my whole heart, promised.   But I wish
to be happy with you—as happy, quite as happy,
as is at all possible, with our best efforts, and
coolest, discreetest management.   I laugh the
matter over sometimes, but I may tell you, since
you are determined to be in earnest, that I have
treated it, in my solitary thought, as the one important event of my life—(so indeed it is !)—and,
as such, worthy of all forethought, patience, self-
denial, and calculation.   To inevitable ills I can
make up my mind like other people.   If your art
were your only hope of subsistence—why—I don't
know—(should I look well as a page ?)—I don't
know that I couldn't run your errands and grind

your paints in hose and doublet. But there is
another door open for you—a counting-house door,
to be sure—leading to opulence and all the appli-
ances of dignity and happiness, and through this
door, my dear Philip, the art you would live by
comes to pay tribute and beg for patronage.
Now, out of your hundred and twenty reasons,
give me the two stoutest and best, why you should
refuse your brother's golden offer of partnership—
my share, in your alternative of poverty, left for
the moment out of the question."

Rather overborne by the confident decision of
his beautiful cousin, and having probably made
up his mind that he must ultimately yield to her,
Philip replied in a lower and more dejected tone :

" If you were not to be a sharer in my renown,
should I be so fortunate as to acquire it, I should
feel as if it were selfish to dwell so much on my
passion for distinction, and my devotion to my
pencil as a means of winning it. My heart is full
of you—but it is full of ambition, too, paradox
though it be. I cannot live ignoble. I should not
have felt worthy to press my love upon you—
worthy to possess you—except with the prospect
of celebrity in my art. You make the world dark
to me, Fanny ! You close down the sky, when
you shut out this hope ! Yet it shall be so."

Philip paused a moment, and the silence was
uninterrupted.

" There was another feeling I had, upon which
I have not insisted," he continued. " By my

brother's project, I am to reside almost wholly abroad. Even the little stipend I have to offer you now is absorbed of course by the investment of my property in his trading capital, and marriage, till I have partly enriched myself, would be even more hopeless than at present. Say the interval were five years—and five years of separation !"

"With happiness in prospect, it would soon pass, my dear Philip !"

"But is there nothing wasted in this time? My life is yours—the gift of love. Are not these coming five years the very flower of it !—a mutual loss, too, for are they not, even more emphatically, the very flower of yours? Eighteen and twenty-five are ages at which to marry, not ages to defer. During this time the entire flow of my existence is at its crowning fulness — passion, thought, joy, tenderness, susceptibility to beauty and sweetness —all I have that can be diminished or tarnished, or made dull by advancing age and contact with the world, is thrown away—for its spring and summer. Will the autumn of life repay us for this? Will it—even if we are rich and blest with health, and as capable of an unblemished union as now? Think of this a moment, dear Fanny !"

"I do—it is full of force and meaning, and, could we marry now, with a tolerable prospect of competency, it would be irresistible. But poverty in wedlock, Philip—"

"What do you call poverty? If we can suffice for each other, and have the necessaries of life, we

are not poor ! My art will bring us consideration
enough—which is the main end of wealth, after all
—and, of society, speaking for myself only, I want
nothing. Luxuries for yourself, Fanny — means
for your dear, comfort and pleasure—you should
not want if the world held them, and surely the un-
bounded devotion of one man to the support of the
one woman he loves, *ought* to suffice for the task !
I am strong—I am capable of labor—I have limbs
to toil, if my genius and my present means fail me,
and, oh, Heaven ! you could not want !"

"No, no, no! I thought not of want !" murmured Miss Bellairs, "I thought only—"

But she was not permitted to finish the sentence.

"Then my bright picture for the future *may* be
realized !" exclaimed Philip, knitting his hands
together in a transport of hope. "I may build up
a reputation, with *you* for the constant partner of
its triumphs and excitements ! I may go through
the world, and have some care in life besides subsistence, how I shall sleep, and eat, and accumulate
gold ; some companion, who, from the threshold
of manhood, shared every thought — and knew
every feeling—some pure and present angel who
walked with me and purified my motives and
ennobled my ambitions, and received from my lips
and eyes, and from the beating of my heart against
her own, all the love I had to give in a lifetime.
Tell me, Fanny ! tell me, my sweet cousin ! is not
this a picture of bliss, which, combined with suc-

cess in my noble art, might make a Paradise on earth for you and me ?''

The hand of Fanny Bellairs rested on the up-turned forehead of her lover as he sat at her feet in the deepening twilight, and she answered him with such sweet words as are linked together by spells known only to woman—but his palette and pencils were, nevertheless, burned in solemn holocaust that very night, and the lady carried her point, as ladies must. And, to the importation of silks from Lyons, was devoted, thenceforth, the genius of a Raphael—perhaps ! Who knows ?

The reader will naturally have gathered from this dialogue that Miss Fanny Bellairs had black eyes, and was rather below the middle stature. She was a belle, and it is only belle-metal of this particular description which is not fusible by ''burning words.'' She had mind enough to appreciate fully the romance and enthusiasm of her cousin, Philip Ballister, and knew precisely the phenomena which a tall *blonde* (this complexion of woman being solu-ble in love and tears) would have exhibited under a similar experiment. While the fire of her love glowed, therefore, she opposed little resistance, and seemed softened and yielding, but her purpose remained unaltered, and she rang out '' No !'' the next morning, with a tone as little changed as a convent-bell from matins to vespers, though it has passed meantime through the furnace of an Italian noon.

Fanny was not a designing girl, either. She might have found a wealthier customer for her heart than her cousin Philip. And she loved this cousin as truly and well as her nature would admit, or as need be, indeed. But two things had conspired to give her the unmalleable quality just described—a natural disposition to confide, first and foremost, on all occasions, in her own sagacity, and a vivid impression made upon her mind by a childhood of poverty. At the age of twelve she had been transferred from the distressed fireside of her mother, Mrs. Bellairs, to the luxurious roof of her aunt, Mrs. Ballister, and, her mother dying soon after, the o.phan girl was adopted, and treated as a child ; but the memory of the troubled hearth at which she had first learned to observe and reason, colored all the purposes and affections, thoughts, impulses, and wishes of the ripening girl, and to think of happiness in any proximity to privation seemed to her impossible, even though it were in the bosom of love. Seeing no reason to give her cousin credit for any knowledge of the world beyond his own experience, she decided to think for him as well as love him, and, not being so much pressed as the enthusiastic painter by the " *besoin d'aimer et de se faire aimer*," she very composedly prefixed, to the possession of her hand, the trifling achievement of getting rich—quite sure that if he knew as much as she, he would willingly run that race without the incumbrance of matrimony.

The death of Mr. Ballister, senior, had left the
widow and her two boys more slenderly provided
for than was anticipated — Phil's portion, after
leaving college, producing the moderate income
before mentioned.   The elder brother had em-
barked in his father's business, and it was thought
best on all hands for the younger Ballister to
follow his example.   But Philip, whose college
leisure had been devoted to poetry and painting,
and whose genius for the latter, certainly, was very
decided, brought down his habits by a resolute
economy to the limits of his income, and took up
the pencil for a profession.   With passionate
enthusiasm, great purity of character, distaste for
all society not in harmony with his favorite pur-
suit, and an industry very much concentrated and
rendered effective by abstemious habits, Philip
Ballister was very likely to develop what genius
might lie between his head and hand, and his progress in the first year had been allowed, by eminent
artists, to give very unusual promise.   The Ballisters were still together, under the maternal roof,
and the painter's studies were the portraits of the
family, and Fanny's picture, of course, much the
most difficult to finish.   It would be very hard if a
painter's portrait of his liege mistress, the lady of
his heart, were not a good picture, and Fanny
Bellairs on canvas was divine accordingly.   If the
copy had more softness of expression than the
original (as it was thought to have), it only proves
that wise men have for some time suspected,

that love is more dumb than blind, and the faults
of our faultless idols are noted, however unconsciously. Neither thumb-screws nor hot coals—
nothing probably but repentance after matrimony
—would have drawn from Philip Ballister, in
words, the same correction of his mistress's foible
that had oozed out through his treacherous pencil !

Cupid is often drawn as a stranger pleading to
be " taken in," but it is a miracle that he is not
invariably drawn as a portrait-painter. A bird tied
to the muzzle of a gun — an enemy who has
written a book—an Indian prince under the protection of Giovanni Bulletto (Tuscan for John
Bull),—is not more close upon demolition, one
would think, than the heart of a lady delivered
over to a painter's eyes, posed, draped, and lighted
with the one object of studying her beauty. If
there be any magnetism in isolated attention, any
in steadfast gazing, any in passes of the hand hither
and thither—if there be any magic in *ce doux demi-
jour* so loved in France, in stuff for flattery ready
pointed and feathered, in freedom of admiration,
" and all in the way of business"—then is a lov-
able sitter to a love-like painter in " parlous"
vicinity (as the new school would phrase it) to
sweet heart-land ! Pleasure in a vocation has no
offset in political economy as honor has (" the more
honor the less profit"), or portrait-painters would
be poorer than poets.

And, *malgré* his consciousness of the quality
which required softening in his cousin's beauty,

and *malgré* his rare advantages for obtaining over her a lover's proper ascendency, Mr. Philip Ballister bowed to the stronger will of Miss Fanny Bellairs, and sailed for France on his apprenticeship to Mammon.

———

The reader will please to advance five years. Before proceeding thence with our story, however, let us take a Parthian glance at the overstepped interval. Philip Ballister had left New York with the triple vow that he would enslave every faculty of his mind and body to business, that he would not return till he had made a fortune, and that such interstices as might occur in the building up of this chateau for felicity should be filled with sweet reveries about Fanny Bellairs. The forsworn painter had genius, as we have before hinted, and genius is (as much as it is any one thing) the power of concentration. He entered upon his duties, accordingly with a force and patience of application which soon made him master of what are called business habits, and, once in possession of the details, his natural cleverness gave him a speedy insight to all the scope and tactics of his particular field of trade. Under his guidance, the affairs of the house were soon in a much more prosperous train, and, after a year's residence at Lyons, Philip saw his way very clear to manage them with a long arm and take up his quarters in Paris. "*Les fats sont les seuls hommes qui aient soin*

d' eux mêmes," says a French novelist, but there is a
period, early or late, in the lives of the cleverest
men, when they become suddenly curious as to
their capacity for the graces. Paris, to a stranger
who does not visit in the Faubourg St. Germain,
is a republic of personal exterior, where the degree of privilege depends, with Utopian impar-
tiality, on the style of the outer man ; and Paris,
therefore, if he is not already a Bachelor of Arts
(qu ?—*beau's Arts*), usually serves the traveller as
an Alma Mater of the pomps and vanities.

Phil. Ballister, up to the time of his matricula-
tion in *Chaussée d' Antin,* was a romantic-looking
sloven. From this to a very dashing coxcomb is
but half a step, and, to be rid of the coxcombry
and retain a look of fashion, is still within the easy
limits of imitation. But—to obtain superiority of
presence, with no apparent aid from dress and no
describable manner, and to display, at the same
time, every natural advantage in effective relief,
and, withal, to adapt this subtle philtre, not only
to the approbation of the critical and censorious,
but to the taste of fair women gifted with judg-
ment as God pleases—this is a finish not born with
any man (though unsuccessful if it do not seem to
be), and never reached in the apprenticeship of
life, and never reached at all by men not much
above their fellows. He who has it, has " bought
his doublet in Italy, his round hose in France, his
bonnet in Germany, and his behavior everywhere,"
for he must know, as a chart of quicksands, the

pronounced models of other nations ; but to be a "picked man of countries," and to *have been* a coxcomb and a man of fashion, are, as a painter would say, but the setting of the palette toward the making of the *chef-d'œuvre.*

Business prospered, and the facilities of leisure increased, while Ballister passed through these transitions of taste, and he found intervals to travel, and time to read, and opportunity to indulge, as far as he could with the eye only, his passion for knowledge in the arts. To all that appertained to the refinement of himself, he applied the fine feelers of a delicate and passionate construction, physical and mental, and, as the reader will already have included, wasted on culture comparatively unprofitable, faculties that would have been better employed but for the meddling of Miss Fanny Bellairs.

———

Ballister's return from France was heralded by the arrival of statuary and pictures, books, furniture, and numberless articles of tasteful and costly luxury. The reception of these by the family at home threw rather a new light on the probable changes in the long-absent brother, for, from the signal success of the business he had managed, they had very naturally supposed that it was the result only of unremitted and plodding care. Vague rumors of changes in his personal appearance had reached them, such as might be expected from con-

formity to foreign fashions, but those who had seen
Philip Ballister in France, and called subsequently
on the family in New York, were not people qualified
to judge of the man, either from their own powers
of observation or from any confidence he was likely
to put forward while in their society. His letters
had been delightful, but they were confined to
third-person topics, descriptions of things likely to
interest them, etc., and Fanny had few addressed
personally to herself, having thought it worth
while, for the experiment sake, or for some other
reason, to see whether love would subsist without
it usual *pabulum* of tender correspondence, and a
veto on love-letters having served her for a parting
injunction at Phil's embarkation for Havre.
However varied by their different fancies, the
transformation looked for by the whole family was
substantially the same—the romantic artist sobered
down to a practical, plain man of business. And
Fanny herself had an occasional misgiving as to
her relish for his counting-house virtues and manners ; though, on the detection of the feeling, she
immediately closed her eyes upon it, and drummed
up her delinquent constancy for " parade and in-
spection."

All bustles are very much alike (we use the word
as defined in Johnson), and the reader will appreciate our delicacy, besides, in not intruding on the
first reunion of relatives and lovers long separated.

The morning after Philip Ballister's arrival, the
family sat long at breakfast. The mother's gaze

fastened untiringly on the features of her son—
still her boy—prying into them with a vain effort
to reconcile the face of the man with the cherished
picture of the child with sunny locks, and noting
little else than the work of inward change upon
the countenance and expression. The brother,
with the predominant feeling of respect for the in-
telligence and industry of one who had made the
fortunes of the house, read only subdued sagacity
in the perfect simplicity of his whole exterior.
And Fanny—Fanny was puzzled. The *bourgeoisie*
and ledger-bred hardness of manner which she had
looked for were not there, nor any variety of the
"foreign slip-slop" common to travelled youth,
nor any superciliousness, nor (faith!) any wear
and tear of youth and good looks—nothing that
she expected — nothing! Not even a French
guard-chain!

What there *was* in her cousin's manners and exterior, however, was much more difficult to define
by Miss Bellairs than what there *was not*. She
began the renewal of their intercourse with very
high spirits, herself—the simple nature and unpre-
tendingness of his address awakening only an unembarrassed pleasure at seeing him again—but she
soon began to suspect there was an exquisite refinement in this very simplicity, and to wonder
"at the trick of it;" and, after the first day
passed in his society, her heart beat when he
spoke to her, as it did not use to beat when she
was sitting to him for her picture, and listening to

his passionate love-making. And, with all her faculties, she studied him. What was the charm of
his presence? He was himself, and himself only.
He seemed perfect, but he seemed to have arrived
at perfection like a statue, not like a picture—by
what had been taken away, not by what had been
laid on. He was as natural as a bird, and as grace-
ful and unembarrassed. He neither forced conversation, nor pressed the little attentions of the
drawing-room, and his attitudes were full of re-
pose; yet she was completely absorbed in what he
said, and she had been impressed imperceptibly
with his high-bred politeness, and the singular
elegance of his person. Fanny felt there was a
change in her relative position to her cousin. In
what it consisted, or which had the advantage, she
was perplexed to discover—but she bit her lips as
she caught herself thinking that if she were not
engaged to marry Philip Ballister, she should suspect that she had just fallen irrecoverably in love
with him.

It would have been a novelty in the history of
Miss Bellairs that any event to which she had once
consented, should admit of reconsideration; and
the Ballister family, used to her strong will, were
confirmed fatalists as to the coming about of her
ends and aims. Her marriage with Philip, therefore, was discussed, *cœur ouvert*, from his first arrival, and, indeed, in her usual fashion of saving
others the trouble of making up their minds, "herself had named the day." This, it is true, was

before his landing, and was, then, an effort of con-
siderable magnanimity, as the expectant Penelope
was not yet advised of her lover's state of preser-
vation or damages by cares and keeping.   If Philip
had not found his wedding-day fixed on his arrival, however, he probably would have had a
voice in the naming of it, for, with Fanny's new
inspirations as to his character, there had grown
up a new flower in her garden of beauties—timid-
ity !   What bird of the air had sown the seed in
such a soil was a problem to herself—but true it
was !—the confident belle had grown a blushing
trembler !   She would as soon have thought of be-
speaking her wings for the sky, as to have ventured
on naming the day in a short week after.

The day *was* named, however, and the preparations went on—*nem. con.*—the person most interested (after herself) accepting every congratulation
and allusion, touching the event, with the most
impenetrable suavity.   The marbles and pictures,
upholstery and services, were delivered over to the
order of Miss Bellairs, and Philip, disposed, apparently, to be very much a recluse in his rooms, or,
at other times, engrossed by troops of welcoming
friends, saw much less of his bride elect than suited
her wishes, and saw her seldom alone.   By particular request, also, he took no part in the plenishing
and embellishing of the new abode—not permitted
even to inquire where it was situated ; and, under
this cover, besides the pleasure of having her own
way, Fanny concealed a little secret, which, when

disclosed, she now felt, would figure forth Philip's comprehension, her whole scheme of future happiness. She had taken the elder brother into her counsels a fortnight after Philip's return, and, with his aid and consent, had abandoned the original idea of a house in town, purchased a beautifully-secluded estate and *cottage ornée*, on the East River, and transferred thither all the objects of art, furniture, etc. One room only of the maternal mansion was permitted to contribute its quota to the completion of the bridal dwelling—the wing, never since inhabited, in which Philip had made his essay as a painter—and, without variation of a cobweb, and, with whimsical care and effort on the part of Miss Fanny, this apartment was reproduced at Revedere —her own picture on the easel, as it stood on the night of his abandonment of his art, and palette, pencils and colors in tempting readiness on the table. Even the fire-grate of the old studio had been re-set in the new, and the cottage throughout had been refitted with a view to occupation in the winter. And to sundry hints on the part of the elder brother, that some thought should be given to a city residence—for the Christmas holidays at least—Fanny replied, through a blush, that she would never wish to see the town—with Philip at ·Revedere !

Five years had ripened and mellowed the beauty of Fanny Bellairs, and the same summer-time of youth had turned into fruit the feeling left by Philip in bud and flower. She was ready now for

love.   She had felt the variable temper of society,
and there was a presentiment in the heart, of receding flatteries and the winter of life.   It was
with mournful self-reproach that she thought of the
years wasted in separation, of her own choosing,
from the man she loved ; and, with the power to
recall time, she would have thanked God with
tears of joy for the privilege of retracing the chain
of life to that link of parting.   Not worth a day of
those lost years, she bitterly confessed to herself,
was the wealth they had purchased.

It lacked as little as one week of " the happy
day," when the workmen were withdrawn from
Revedere, and the preparations for a family breakfast, to be succeeded by the agreeable surprise to
Philip of informing him he was at home, were
finally completed.   One or two very intimate
friends were added to the party, and the invitations
(from the elder Ballister) proposed simply a *déjeuner
sur l'herbe* in the grounds of an unoccupied villa,
the property of an acquaintance.

With the subsiding of the excitement of return,
the early associations which had temporarily con-
fused and colored the feelings of Philip Ballister
settled gradually away, leaving uppermost once
more the fastidious refinement of the Parisian.
Through this medium, thin and cold, the bubbles
from the breathing of the heart of youth, rose
rarely and reluctantly.   The Ballisters held a good
station in society, without caring for much beyond
the easy conveniences of life, and Fanny, though

capable of any degree of elegance, had not seen
the expediency of raising the tone of her manners
above that of her immediate friends. Without
being positively distasteful to Philip, the family
circle, Fanny included, left him much to desire in
the way of society, and, unwilling to abate the
warmth of his attentions while with them, he had
latterly pleaded occupation more frequently, and
passed his time in the more congenial company of
his library of art. This was the less noticed that it
gave Miss Bellairs the opportunity to make fre-
quent visits to the workmen at Revedere, and, in
the polished devotion of her betrothed when with
her, Fanny saw nothing reflected but her own daily
increasing tenderness and admiration.

The morning of the *fête* came in like the air in an
overture—a harmony of all the instruments of
summer. The party were at the gate of Revedere
by ten, and the drive through the avenue to the
lawn drew a burst of delighted admiration from
all. The place was exquisite, and seen in its
glory, and Fanny's heart was brimming with
gratified pride and exultation. She assumed at
once the dispensation of the honors, and beautiful
she looked with her snowy dress and raven ring-
lets flitting across the lawn, and queening it like
Perdita among the flowers. Having narrowly
escaped bursting into tears of joy when Philip pronounced the place prettier than anything he had
seen in his travels, she was, for the rest of the day,
calmly happy ; and, with the grateful shade, the

delicious breakfast in the grove, the rambling and boating on the river, the hours passed off like dreams, and no one even hinted a regret that the house itself was under lock and bar. And so the sun set, and the twilight came on, and the guests were permitted to order round their carriages and depart, the Ballisters accompanying them to the gate. And, on the return of the family through the avenue, excuses were made for idling hither and thither, till light began to show through the trees, and, by the time of their arrival at the lawn, the low windows of the cottage poured forth streams of light, and the open doors, and servants busy within, completed a scene more like magic than reality. Philip was led in by the excited girl who was the fairy of the spell, and his astonishment at the discovery of his statuary and pictures, books and furniture, arranged in complete order within, was fed upon with the passionate delight of love in authority.

When an hour had been spent in examining and admiring the different apartments, an inner room was thrown open, in which supper was prepared, and this fourth act in the day's drama was lingered over in untiring happiness by the family.

Mrs. Ballister, the mother, rose and retired, and Philip pleaded indisposition, and begged to be shown to the room allotted to him. This was ringing-up the curtain for the last act sooner than had been planned by Fanny, but she announced herself as his chamberlain, and, with her hands affectionately crossed on his arm, led him to a suite of rooms in a wing still unvisited, and, with a good-night kiss, left him at the open door of the revived studio, furnished for the night with a bachelor's bed. Turning upon the threshold, he closed the door with a parting wish of sweet dreams, and Fanny, after listening a moment with a vain hope of overhearing some expression of pleasure, and lingering again on her way back, to be overtaken by her surprised lover, sought her own bed without rejoining the circle, and passed a sleepless and happy night of tears and joy.

Breakfast was served the next morning on a terrace overlooking the river, and it was voted by acclamation that Fanny never before looked so lovely. As none but the family were to be present, she had stolen a march on her marriage wardrobe, and added to her demi-toilet a morning cap of exquisite becomingness. Altogether she looked deliciously wife-like, and did the honors of the breakfast-table with a grace and sweetness that warmed out love and compliments even from the sober soil of household intimacy. Philip had not yet made his appearance, and they lingered long at table, till at last, a suggestion that he might be ill started Fanny to her feet, and she ran to his door before a servant could be summoned.

The rooms were open, and the bed had not been occupied. The candle was burned to the socket, and on the easel, resting against the picture, was a letter addressed—" Miss Fanny Bellairs."

THE LETTER.

" I have followed up to this hour, my fair cousin, in the path you have marked out for me. It has brought me back, in this chamber, to the point from which I started under your guidance, and if it had brought me back unchanged — if it restored me my energy, my hope, and my prospect of fame, I should pray Heaven that it would also give me back my love, and be content—more than content, if it gave me back also my poverty. The sight of my easel, and of the surroundings of my boyish dreams of glory, have made my heart bitter. They have given form and voice to a vague unhappiness, which has haunted me through all these absent years—years of degrading pursuits and wasted powers—and it now impels me from you, kind and lovely as you are, with an aversion I cannot control. I cannot forgive you. You have thwarted my destiny. You have extinguished with sordid cares a lamp within me, that might, by this time, have shone through the world. And what am I, since your wishes are accomplished? Enriched in pocket, and bankrupt in happiness and self-respect.

" With a heart sick, and a brain aching for distinction, I have come to an unhonored stand-still at thirty! I am a successful tradesman, and in this character I shall probably die. Could I begin to be a painter now, say you? Alas! my knowledge of the art is too great for patience with the slow hand ! I could not draw a line without de-spair. The pliant fingers and the plastic mind must keep pace to make progress in art. My taste is fixed, and my imagination uncreative, because chained down by certainties ; and the shortsighted ardor and daring experiments which are indispen-sable to sustain and advance the follower in Raph-ael's footsteps, are too far behind for my resum-ing. The tide ebbed from me at the accursed burning of my pencils by your pitiless hand, and from that hour I have felt hope receding. Could I be happy with you, stranded here in ignoble idle-ness, and owing to you the loss of my whole vent-ure of opportunity ? No, Fanny ?—surely no !

" I would not be unnecessarily harsh. I am sen-sible of your affection and constancy. I have de-ferred this explanation unwisely, till the time and place make it seem more cruel. You are at this very moment, I well know, awake in your cham-ber, devoting to me the vigils of a heart overflow-ing with tenderness. And I would—if it were pos-sible—if it were not utterly beyond my powers of self-sacrifice and concealment—I would affect a devotion I cannot feel, and carry out this error through a life of artifice and monotony. But here, again, the work is your own, and my feelings re-vert bitterly to your interference. If there were no other obstacle to my marrying you—if you were not associated repulsively with the dark cloud on my life, you are not the woman I could now en-

throne in my bosom. We have diverged since the
separation which I pleaded against, and which you
commanded. I need for my idolatry, now, a creature to whom the sordid cares you have sacrificed
me to, are utterly unknown—a woman born and
educated in circumstances where want is never
feared, and where calculation never enters. I
must lavish my wealth, if I fulfil my desire, on
one who accepts it like the air she breathes, and
who knows the value of nothing but love—a bird
with a human soul and form, believing herself free
of all the world is rich in, and careful only for
pleasure and the happiness of those who belong to
her. Such women, beautiful and highly educated,
are found only in ranks of society between which
and my own I have been increasing in distance—
nay, building an impassable barrier, in obedience
to your control. Where I stop, interdicted by the
stain of trade, the successful artist is free to enter.
You have stamped me *plebeian*—you would not
share my slow progress toward a higher sphere,
and you have disqualified me for attaining it
alone. In your mercenary and immovable will,
and in that only, lies the secret of our twofold
unhappiness.

" I leave you, to return to Europe. My brother
and my friends will tell you I am mad and inex-
cusable, and look upon you as a victim. They will
say that, to have been a painter, were nothing to
the career that I might mark out for my ambition,
if ambition I must have, in politics. Politics in a

country where distinction is a pillory! But I
could not live here. It is my misfortune that my
tastes are so modified by that long and compul-
sory exile, that life, here, would be a perpetual
penance. This unmixed air of merchandise suffo-
cates me. Our own home is tinctured black with
it. You yourself, in this rural Paradise you have
conjured up, move in it like a cloud. The counting-house rings in your voice, calculation draws
together your brows, you look on everything as
a *means*, and know its cost ; and the calm and
means-forgetting *fruition*, which forms the charm
and dignity of superior life, is utterly unknown to
you. What would be my happiness with such a
wife ? What would be yours with such a husband ?
Yet I consider the incompatibility between us as
no advantage on my part—on the contrary, a punishment, and of your inflicting. What shall I be,
anywhere, but a Tantalus — a fastidious *ennuyé*,
with a thirst for the inaccessible burning in my
bosom continually !

" I pray you let us avoid another meeting before
my departure. Though I cannot forgive you as a
lover, I can think of you with pleasure as a cousin,
and I give you as your due ('damages,' the law
would phrase it,) the portion of myself which you
thought most important when I offered you my
all. You would not take me without the fortune,
but perhaps you will be content with the fortune
without me. I shall immediately take steps to

convey to you this property of Revedere, with an income sufficient to maintain it, and I trust soon to hear that you have found a husband better worthy of you than your cousin—

"PHILIP BALLISTER."

FRIEND BARTON'S CONCERN.

BY MARY HALLOCK FOOTE.

I T had been " borne in" upon him, more or less,
during the long winter ; it had not relaxed its
hold when the frosts unlocked and the streams
were set free from their long winter's silence among
the hills. He grew restless and abstracted under
" the turnings of the Lord's hand upon him," and
his speech unconsciously shaped itself into the
Biblical cadences which came to him in his moments of spiritual exercise.

The bedrabbled snows of March shrank away
before the keen, quickening sunbeams ; the hills
emerged, brown and sodden, like the chrysalis of
the new year. The streams woke in a tumult, and
all day and night their voices called from the hills
back of the mill. The waste-weir was a foaming
torrent, and spread itself in muddy shallows across
the meadow beyond the old garden where the rob-

ins and blue birds were house-hunting. Friend
Barton's trouble stirred with the life-blood of the
year, and pressed upon him sorely ; but as yet he
gave it no words. He plodded about among his
lean kine, tempering the winds of March to his un-
timely lambs, and reconciling unnatural ewes to
their maternal duties.

Friend Barton had never heard of the doctrine
of the survival of the fittest ; though it was the
spring of 1812, and England and America were
investigating the subject on the seas, while the
nations of Europe were practically illustrating it.
The "hospital tent," as the boys called an old
corn-basket, covered with carpet, which stood beside the kitchen chimney, was seldom without an
occupant,—a brood of chilled chickens, a weakly
lamb, or a wee pig (with too much blue in its pink-
ness), which had been left behind by its stouter
brethren in the race for existence. The old mill
hummed away through the day, and often late in
the evening if time pressed, upon the grists which
added a thin, intermittent stream of tribute to the
family income. Whenever work was "slack,"
Friend Barton was sawing or chopping in the
wood-shed adjoining the kitchen ; every moment
he could seize or make he was there, stooping over
the rapidly growing pile.

"Seems to me, father, thee's in a great hurry
with the wood this spring. I don't know when
we've had such a pile ahead."

" 'Twon't burn up any faster for being chopped,"

Friend Barton said ; and then his wife Rachel knew that if he had a reason for being "forehanded" with the wood, he was not ready to give it.

One rainy April afternoon, when the smoky gray distances began to take a tinge of green, and through the drip and rustle of the rain the call of the robins sounded, Friend Barton sat in the door of the barn, oiling the road-harness. The old chaise had been wheeled out and greased, and its cushions beaten and dusted.

An ox-team with a load of grain creaked up the hill and stopped at the mill door. The driver, seeing Friend Barton's broad-brimmed drab felt hat against the dark interior of the barn, came down the short lane leading from the mill past the house and farm-buildings.

"Fixin' up for travellin', Uncle Tommy ?"

Vain compliments were unacceptable to Thomas Barton, and he was generally known and addressed as "Uncle Tommy" by the world's people of a younger generation.

"It is not in man that walketh to direct his own steps, neighbor Gordon. I am getting myself in readiness to obey the Lord, whichever way He calls me."

Farmer Gordon cast a shrewd eye over the premises. They wore that patient, sad, exhumed look which old farm-buildings are apt to have in early spring. The roofs were black with rain, and brightened with patches of green moss. Farmer Gordon instinctively calculated how many "bunches o' shingle" would be required to rescue them from the decline into which they had fallen, in spite of the hectic green spots.

"Wal, the Lord calls most of us to stay at home and look after things, such weather as this. Good plantin' weather; good weather for breakin' ground; fust-rate weather for millin'! This is a reg'lar miller's rain, Uncle Tommy. You ought to be takin' advantage of it. I've got a grist back here; wish ye could manage to let me have it when I come back from store."

The grist was ground and delivered before Friend Barton went in to his supper that night. Dorothy Barton had been mixing bread, and was wiping her white arms and hands on the roller towel by the kitchen door, as her father stamped and scraped his feet on the stones outside.

"I do believe I forgot to toll neighbor Gordon's rye," he said, as he gave a final rub on the broom Dorothy handed out to him. "It's wonderful how careless I get!"

"Well, father, I don't suppose thee'd ever forget, and toll a grist twice!"

"I believe I've been mostly preserved from mistakes of that kind," said Friend Barton gently. "It may have been the Lord who stayed my hand from gathering profit unto myself while his lambs go unfed."

Dorothy put her hands on her father's shoulders. She was almost as tall as he, and could look into his patient, troubled eyes.

" Father, I know what thee is thinking of ; but do think *long*. It will be a hard year ; the boys *ought* to go to school ; and mother is so feeble."

Friend Barton's " concern" kept him awake long that night. His wife watched by his side, giving no sign, lest her wakeful presence should disturb his silent wrestlings. The tall, cherry-wood clock in the entry measured the hours as they passed with its slow, dispassionate tick.

At two o'clock Rachel Barton was awakened from her first sleep of weariness by her husband's voice whispering heavily in the darkness.

" My way is hedged up ! I see no way to go forward. Lord, strengthen my patience, that I murmur not, after all I have seen of Thy goodness. I find daily bread is very desirable ; want and necessity are painful to nature ; but shall I follow Thee for the sake of the loaves, or will it do to forsake Thee in times of emptiness and abasement ?"

There was silence again, and restless tossings and sighings continued the struggle.

" Thomas," the wife's voice spoke tremulously in the darkness, " my dear husband, I know where thy thoughts are tending. If the Spirit is with thee, do not deny it for our sakes, I pray thee. The Lord did not give thee thy wife and children to hang as a millstone round thy neck. I am thy helpmeet, to strengthen thee in his service. I am thankful that I have my health this spring better than usual, and Dorothy is a wonderful help. Her spirit was sent to sustain me in thy long absences.

Go, dear, and serve our Master, who has called
thee in these bitter strivings ! Dorothy and I will
keep things together as well as we can. The way
will open—never fear !" She put out her hand
and touched his face in the darkness ; there were
tears on the furrowed cheeks. " Try to sleep,
dear, and let thy spirit have rest. There is but
one answer to this call."

With the first drowsy twitterings of the birds,
when the crescent-shaped openings in the board
shutters began to define themselves clearly in the
shadowy room, they arose and went about their
morning tasks in silence. Friend Barton's step
was a little heavier than usual, and the hollows
round his wife's pale brown eyes were a little
deeper. As he sat on the splint-bottomed chair by
the kitchen fireplace, drawing on his boots, she
laid her hands on his shoulders, and her cheek on
the worn spot on the top of his head.

" Thee will lay this concern before meeting to-
morrow, father ?"

" I had it on my mind to do so,—if my light be
not quenched before then."

Friend Barton's light was not quenched. Words
came to him without seeking, in which to " open
the concern which had ripened in his mind," of a
religious visit to the meeting constituting the
yearly meetings of Philadelphia and Baltimore.
A " minute" was given him encouraging him in
the name of, and with the full concurrence of, the
monthly meetings of Nine Partners, and Stony

Valley, to go wherever the Truth might lead him.
While Friend Barton was thus freshly anointed,
and "abundantly encouraged," his wife, Rachel,
was talking with Dorothy in the low upper chamber, known as the "wheel-room."

Dorothy was spinning wool on the big wheel,
dressed in her light calico short-gown and brown
quilted petticoat ; her arms were bare, and her hair
was gathered away from her flushed cheeks and
knotted behind her ears. The roof sloped down
on one side, and the light came from a long low
window under the eaves. There was another window (shaped like a half moon high up in the peak),
but it sent down only one long beam of sunlight,
which glimmered across the dust and fell upon
Dorothy's white neck.

The wheel was humming a quick measure, and
Dorothy trod lightly back and forth, the wheel-
pin in one hand, the other upraised holding the
tense, lengthening thread, which the spindle de-
voured again.

"Dorothy, thee looks warm :—can't thee sit
down a moment, while I talk to thee ?"

"Is it anything important, mother ? I want to
get my twenty knots before dinner." She paused
as she joined a long tress of wool at the spindle.
"Is it anything about father ?"

"Yes, it's about father, and all of us."

"I know," said Dorothy, stretching herself back
with a sigh. "He's going away again !"

"Yes, dear. He feels that he is called. It is a

time of trouble and contention everywhere,—' the harvest truly is plenteous, but the laborers are few.' "

"There are not so *many* 'laborers' *here*, mother, though to be sure, the harvest—"

"Dorothy, my daughter! don't let a spirit of levity creep into thy speech. Thy father has striven and wrestled with his urgings. I've seen it working on him all winter; he feels now it is the Lord's will."

"I don't see how he can be so sure," said Dorothy, swaying gloomily to and fro against the wheel. "I don't care for myself,—I'm not afraid of work,—but *thee's* not able to do what thee does *now*, mother. If I have outside things to look after, how can I help thee as I should? The boys are about as much dependence as a flock of barn swallows!"

"Don't fret about me, dear; the way will open. Thy father has thought and planned for us; have patience while I tell thee. Thee knows Walter Evesham's pond is small and his mill is doing a thriving business?'

"Yes, I know it!" Dorothy exclaimed. "He has his own share, and ours too—most of it!"

"Wait, dear, wait! Thy father has rented him the ponds to use when his own gives out. He is to have the control of the water, and it will give us a little income, even though the old mill does stand idle."

"He may as well take the mill, too. If father is

away all summer it will be useless ever to start it
again. Thee'll see, mother, how it will end if
Walter Evesham has the custom and the water all
summer. I think it's miserable for a young man
to be so keen about money."

"Dorothy, seems to me thee's hasty in thy judg-
ments. I never heard that said of Walter Evesham. His father left him with capital to improve
his mill. It does better work than ours; we can't
complain of that. Thy father was never one to
study much after ways of making money. He felt
he had no right to more than an honest livelihood.
I don't say that Walter Evesham's in the wrong.
We know that Joseph took advantage of his oppor-
tunities, though I can't say that I ever felt much
unity with some of his transactions. What would
thee have, my dear? Thee's discouraged with
thy father for choosing the thorny way, which we
tread with him; but thee seems no better satisfied
with one who considers the flesh and its wants!"

"I don't *know*, mother, *what* I want for myself.
It doesn't matter, but for thee I would have rest
from all these cruel worries thee has borne so
long."

She buried her face in her mother's lap and put
her strong young arms about the frail, toil-bent
form.

"There, there, dear. Try to rule thy spirit,
Dorothy. Thee's too much worked up about this.
They are not worries to me. I am thankful we
have nothing to decide, one way or the other—only

to do our best with what is given us. Thee's not
thyself, dear. Go down-stairs and fetch in the
clothes, and don't hurry ; stay out till thee gets
more composed.''

Dorothy did not succeed in bringing herself into
unity with her father's call, but she came to a fuller
realization of his struggle. When he bade them
good-by, his face showed what it had cost him,
but Rachel was calm and cheerful. The pain of
parting is keenest to those who go, but it stays
longer with those who are left behind.

'' Dorothy, take good care of thy mother !''
Friend Barton said, taking his daughter's face
between his hands and gravely kissing her brow
between the low-parted ripples of her hair.

'' Yes, father,'' she said, looking into his eyes.
'' Thee knows I'm thy eldest son.''

They watched the old chaise swing round the
corner of the lane, then the pollard willows shut
it from sight.

'' Come, mother,'' said Dorothy, hurrying her in
at the gate. '' I'm going to make a great pot of
mush, and have it hot for supper, and fried for
breakfast, and warmed up with molasses for dinner, and there'll be some cold with milk for supper, and we shan't have any cooking to do at all.''

They went round to the kitchen door. Rachel
stopped in the wood-shed, and the tears rushed to
her eyes.

'' Dear father ! How he has worked over that
wood, early and late, to spare us !''

We will not revive Dorothy's struggles with the farm-work and with the boys. They were an isolated family at the mill-house ; their peculiar faith isolated them still more, and they were twelve miles from meeting and the settlement of Friends at Stony Valley. Dorothy's pride kept her silent about her needs, lest they might bring reproach upon her father among the neighbors, who would not be likely to feel the urgency of his spiritual summons.

The summer heats came on apace and the nights grew shorter. It seemed to Dorothy that she had hardly stretched out her tired young body and forgotten her cares in the low attic bedroom, before the east was streaked with light and the birds were singing in the apple-trees, whose falling blossoms drifted in at the window.

One day in early June, Friend Barton's flock of sheep—consisting of nine experienced ewes, six yearlings, and a sprinkling of close-curled lambs whose legs had not yet come into mature relations with their bodies—were gathered in a little railed inclosure, beside the stream which flowed into the " mill-head." It was supplied by the waste from the pond, and when the gate was shut, rambled easily over the gray slate pebbles, with here and there a fall, just forcible enough to serve as a douche bath for a well-grown sheep. The victims were panting in their heavy fleeces, and their hoarse, plaintive tremolo mingled with the ripple of the water and the sound of young voices in a frolic. Dorothy had divided her forces for the washing to the best advantage. The two elder boys stood in the stream to receive the sheep, which she, with the help of little Jimmy, caught and dragged to the bank.

The boys were at work now upon an elderly ewe, while Dorothy stood on the brink of the stream, braced against an ash sapling, dragging at the fleece of a beautiful but reluctant yearling. Her bare feet were incased in a pair of moccasins which laced around the ankle ; her petticoats were kilted, and her broad hat bound down with a ribbon ; one sleeve was rolled up, the other had been sacrificed in a scuffle in the sheep-pen. The new candidate for immersion stood bleating and trembling, with her fore feet planted against the slippery bank, pushing back with all her strength, while Jimmy propelled from the rear.

" Boys !" Dorothy's clear voice called across the stream. " *Do* hurry ! She's been in long enough, now ! Keep her head up, can't you, and squeeze the wool *hard!* You're not *half* washing ! Oh, Reuby ! thee'll drown her ! Keep her *head* up !"

Another unlucky douse and another half-smothered bleat,—Dorothy released the yearling and plunged to the rescue. " Go after that lamb, Reuby !" she cried, with exasperation in her voice. Reuby followed the yearling, which had disappeared over the orchard slope, upsetting an obstacle in its path, which happened to be Jimmy. He was now wailing on the bank, while Dorothy, with the ewe's nose tucked comfortably in the bend of her arm, was parting and squeezing the fleece, with the water swirling round her. Her stout arms ached, and her ears were stunned with the incessant bleating ; she counted with dismay the sheep still waiting in the pen. " Oh, Jimmy ! *do* stop crying, or else go to the house !''

" He'd better go after Reuby,'' said Sheppard Barton, who was now Dorothy's sole dependence.

" Oh yes ; do, Jimmy, that's a good boy. Tell him to let the yearling go, and come back quick.''

The water had run low that morning in Evesham's pond. He shut down the mill, and strode up the hills, across lots, to raise the gate of the lower Barton Pond, which had been heading up for his use. He passed the corn-field where, a month before, he had seen pretty Dorothy Barton dropping corn with her brothers. It made him ache to think of Dorothy, with her feeble mother, the boys, as wild as preacher's sons proverbially are, and the old farm running down on her hands ; the fences all needed mending, and there went Reuben Barton, now, careering over the fields in chase of a stray yearling. His mother's house was big, and lonely, and empty ; and he flushed as he thought of the " one ewe-lamb'' he coveted, out of Friend Barton's rugged pastures. As he raised the gate, and leaned to watch the water swirl and gurgle through the " trunk,'' sucking the long weeds with it, and thickening with its tumult the clear current

of the stream, the sound of voices and bleating of
sheep came up from below. He had not the farm-
ing instincts in his blood ;—the distant bleating,
the hot June sunshine and cloudless sky, did not
suggest to him sheep-washing ;—but now came a
boy's voice shouting and a cry of distress, and he
remembered, with a thrill, that Friend Barton used
the stream for that peaceful purpose. He shut
down the gate and tore along through the ferns
and tangled grass till he came to the sheep-pen,
where the bank was muddy and trampled. The
prisoners were bleating drearily and looking with
longing eyes across to the other side, where those
who had suffered were now straying and cropping
the short turf, through the lights and shadows of
the orchard.

There was no other sign of life, except a broad
hat with a brown ribbon, buffeted about in an
eddy, among the stones. The stream dipped now
below the hill, and the current, still racing fast with
the impetus he had given it, shot away among the
hazel thickets which crowded close to the brink.
He was obliged to make a detour by the orchard,
and come out at the " mill-head " below ;—a black,
deep pool, with an ugly ripple setting across it to
the " head-gate." He saw something white cling-
ing there and ran round the brink. It was the sodden fleece of the old ewe which had been drifted
against the " head-gate," and held there to her
death. Evesham, with a sickening contraction of
the heart, threw off his jacket for a plunge, when

Dorothy's voice called rather faintly from the willows on the opposite bank.

"Don't jump! I'm here," she said. Evesham searched the willows, and found her seated in the sun just beyond, half buried in a bed of ferns.

"I wouldn't have called thee," she said shyly, as he sank, pale and panting, beside her, "but thee looked—I thought thee was going to jump into the mill-head!"

"I thought *you* were there, Dorothy!"

"I was there quite long enough. Shep pulled me out; I was too tired to help myself much." Dorothy held her palm pressed against her temple, and the blood trickled from beneath, streaking her pale, wet cheek.

"He's gone to the house to get me a cloak. I don't want mother to see me—not yet," she said.

"I'm afraid you ought not to wait, Dorothy. Let me take you to the house, won't you? I'm afraid you'll get a deadly chill."

Dorothy did not look in the least like death. She was blushing now, because Evesham would think it so strange of her to stay, and yet she could not rise in her wet clothes, which clung to her like the calyx to a bud.

"Let me see that cut, Dorothy, *please!*"

"Oh, it's nothing. I don't *wish* thee to look at it!"

"But I will! Do you want to make me your murderer—sitting there in your wet clothes, with a cut on your head?"

He drew away her hand, and the wound, indeed, was no great affair, but he bound it up deftly with strips of his handkerchief. Dorothy's wet curls touched his fingers and clung to them, and her eyelashes drooped lower and lower.

"I think it was *very* stupid of thee. Didn't thee hear us from the dam? I'm sure we made noise enough."

"Yes, I heard you when it was too late. I heard the sheep before, but how could I imagine that *you*, Dorothy, and three boys, as big as cockerels, were sheep-washing? It's the most preposterous thing I ever heard of!"

"Well, I can't help being a woman, and the sheep had to be washed. I think there ought to be more men in the world when half of them are preaching and fighting."

"If you'd only let the men who are left help you a little, Dorothy!"

"I don't want any help. I only *don't* want to be washed into the mill-head."

They both laughed, and Evesham began again entreating her to let him take her to the house.

"Hasn't thee a coat or something I could put around me until Shep comes?" said Dorothy. "He must be here soon."

"Yes, I've got a jacket here somewhere."

He sped away to find it, and faithless Dorothy, as the willows closed beween them, sprang to her feet and fled like a startled Naiad to the house.

When Evesham, pushing through the willows, saw nothing but the bed of wet, crushed ferns and the trail through the long grass where Dorothy's feet had fled, he smiled grimly to himself, remembering that "ewe-lambs" are not always as meek as they look.

That evening Rachel had received a letter from Friend Barton, and was preparing to read it aloud to the children. They were in the kitchen, where the boys had been helping Dorothy, in a desultory manner, to shell corn for the chickens; but now all was silence, while Rachel wiped her glasses and turned the large sheet of paper, squared with many foldings, to the candle.

She read the date, "London Grove, 5th month, 22nd.—Most affectionately beloved." "He means us all," said Rachel, turning to the children with a tender smile. "It's spelled with a small b."

"He means thee!" said Dorothy, laughing. "Thee's not such a very big beloved."

There was a moment's silence. "I don't know that the opening of the letter is of general interest," Rachel mused, with her eyes travelling slowly down the page. "He says: 'In regard to my health, lest thee should concern thyself, I am thankful to say I have never enjoyed better since years have made me acquainted with my infirmities of body, and I earnestly hope that my dear wife and children are enjoying the same blessing.

"'I trust the boys are not deficient in obedience and helpfulness. At Sheppard's age I had already

begun to take the duties of a man upon my shoulders.' ''

Sheppard giggled uncomfortably, and Dorothy
laughed outright.

" Oh ! if father only *knew* how good the boys
are ! Mother, thee must write and tell him about
their ' helpfulness and obedience ' ! Thee can tell
him their appetites keep up pretty well ; they manage to take their meals regularly, and they 'are
always out of bed by eight o'clock, to help me hang
up the milking-stool !''

" Just wait till thee gets in the mill-head again,
Dorothy Barton ! Thee needn't come to *me* to
help thee out !''

" Go on, mother ! Don't let the boys interrupt
thee !''

" Well,'' said Rachel, rousing herself, " where
was I ? Oh, ' when I was Sheppard's age ' : Well,
next come some allusions to the places where he
has visited, and his spiritual exercises there. I
don't know that the boys are quite old enough to
enter into this yet. Thee'd better read it thyself,
Dorothy. I'm keeping all father's letters for the
boys to read, when they are old enough to appreciate them.''

" Well, I think thee might read us about where
he's been preachin' ! We can understand a great
deal more than thee thinks we can !'' said Shep, in
an injured voice. " Reuby, he can preach some
himself ! Thee ought to hear him, mother. It's
almost as good as meetin' !''

"I *wondered* how Reuby spent his time!" said Dorothy, and the mother hastened to interpose.

"Well, here's a passage that may be interesting : 'On sixth day attended the youths' meeting here, —a pretty favored time on the whole. Joseph ' [that's Joseph Carpenter ; he mentions him aways back] 'had good service in lively testimony, while I was calm and easy, without a word to say. At a meeting at Plumstead, we suffered long, but at length we felt relieved. The unfaithful were admonished, the youth invited, and the heavy-hearted encouraged. It was a heavenly time !' Heretofore he seems to have been closed up with silence a good deal ; but now the way opens continually for him to free himself. He's been ' much favored,' he says, ' of late.' Reuby, what's thee doing to thy brothers ?" (Shep and Reuby, who had been persecuting Jimmy by pouring handfuls of corn down the neck of his jacket until he had taken refuge behind Dorothy's chair, were now recriminating with corn-cobs on each other's faces.) " Dorothy, can't thee keep those boys quiet ?"

" Did thee ever know them to be quiet ?" said Dorothy, helping Jimmy to relieve himself of his corn.

" Well now, listen !" Rachel continued placidly, " ' Second day, 27th ' (of fifth month, he means, the letter's been a *long time* coming), ' attended their mid-week meeting at London Grove, where my tongue as it were clave to the roof of my mouth, while Hannah Husbands was much favored, and, enabled to lift up her voice like the song of an angel ' ''—

" Who's Hannah Husbands ?'' cried Dorothy.

" Thee don't know her, dear. She was second cousin to thy father's step-mother ; the families were not congenial, I believe ; but she has a great gift for the ministry.''

" I should think she'd better be at home with her children,—if she has any. Fancy *thee*, mother, going about to strange meetings, and lifting up thy voice.''

" Hush ! hush ! Dorothy ! Thy tongue's running away with thee. Consider the example thee's setting the boys.''

" Thee'd better write to father about Dorothy, mother ! Perhaps Hannah Husbands would like to know what she thinks about her preachin' !''

" Well now, be quiet, all of you. Here's something about Dorothy : ' I know that my dear daughter Dorothy is faithful and loving, albeit somewhat quick of speech, and restive under obligation. I would have thee remind her that an unwillingness to accept help from others argues a want of Christian Meekness. Entreat her, from me, not to conceal her needs from our neighbors, if so be she find her work oppressive. We know them to be of kindly intention, though not of our way of thinking in all particulars. Let her receive help from them, not as individuals, but as instruments of the Lord's protection, which it were impiety and ingratitude to deny.' ''

" There !" cried Shep. " That means thee's to let Luke Jordan finish the sheep-washing. Thee'd better have done it in the first place. We wouldn't have the old ewe to pick if thee had !"

Dorothy was dimpling at the idea of Luke Jordan in the character of an instrument of heavenly protection. She had not regarded him in that light, it must be confessed, and had rejected him with scorn.

" He may if he wants to," she said ; " but you boys shall drive them over. I'll have nothing to do with it."

" And shear them too, Dorothy ? He asked to shear them long ago."

" Well, *let* him shear them, and keep the wool too."

" I wouldn't say that, Dorothy !" said Rachel Barton. " We need the wool, and it seems as if over-payment might not be quite honest either."

" Oh ! mother, mother ! What a mother thee is !" cried Dorothy laughing, and rumpling her cap-strings in a tumultuous embrace.

" She's a great deal too good for *thee*, Dorothy Barton."

" She's too good for all of us ! How did thee ever come to have such a graceless set of children, mother ?"

" I'm very well satisfied," said Rachel. " But now do be quiet, and let's finish the letter. We must get to bed some time to-night !"

The wild clematis was in blossom now—the

fences were white with it, and the rusty cedars
were crowned with virgin wreaths, but the weeds
were thick in the garden and in the potato patch.
Dorothy, stretching her cramped back, looked
longingly up the shadowy vista of the farm-lane,
which had nothing to do but ramble off into the
remotest green fields, where the daisies' faces were
as white and clear as in early June.

One hot August night she came home late from
the store. The stars were thick in the sky ; the
katydids made the night oppressive with their
rasping questionings, and a hoarse revel of frogs
kept the ponds from falling asleep in the shadow
of the hills.

"Is thee very tired to-night, Dorothy ?" her
mother asked, as she took her seat on the low step
of the porch. "Would thee mind turning old
John out thyself ?"

"No, mother, I'm not tired. But why—oh, *I*
know !" cried Dorothy, with a quick laugh.
"The dance—at Slocum's barn. I *thought* those
boys were uncommonly helpful."

"Yes, dear, it's but natural they should want to
see it. Hark ! we can hear the music from here."

They listened, and the breeze brought across the
fields the sound of fiddles and the rhythmic tramp
of feet, softened by the distance. Dorothy's
young pulses leaped.

"Mother, is it any harm for them just to *see* it ?
They have so little fun except what they get out of
teasing and shirking."

" My dear, thy father would never countenance such a scene of frivolity, or permit one of his children to look upon it."

Through our eyes and ears the world takes possession of our hearts.

" Then I'm to spare the boys this temptation, mother? Thee will trust *me* to pass the barn ?"

" I would trust my boys, if they were thy age Dorothy. But their resolution is tender, like their years."

It might be questioned whether the frame of mind in which the boys went to bed that night, under their mother's eye,—for Rachel could be firm in a case of conscience,—was more improving than the frivolity of Slocum's barn.

" Mother," called Dorothy, looking in at the kitchen window, where Rachel was stooping over the embers in the fireplace, to light a bedroom candle, " I want to speak to thee."

Rachel came to the window, screening the candle with her hand.

" Will thee trust *me* to look at the dancing a little while ? It is so very near."

" Why, Dorothy, does thee *want* to ?"

" Yes, mother, I believe I do. I've never seen a dance in my life. It cannot ruin me to look just once."

Rachel stood puzzled.

" Thee's old enough to judge for thyself, Dorothy. But, my child, do not tamper with thy inclinations through heedless curiosity. Thee knows thee's more impulsive than I could wish—for thy own peace.''

" I'll be very careful, mother. If I feel in the *least* wicked I will not look.''

She kissed her mother's hand, which rested on the window-sill. Rachel did not like the kiss, or Dorothy's brilliant eyes and flushed cheeks, as the candle revealed them like a fair picture painted on the darkness. She hesitated, and Dorothy sped away up the lane with old John lagging at his halter.

Was it the music growing nearer that quickened her breathing, or only the closeness of the night, shut in between the wild grape-vine curtains, swung from one dark cedar column to another? She caught the sweet-brier breath as she hurried by, and now, a loop in the leafy curtain revealed the pond lying black in a hollow of the hills, with a whole heaven of stars reflected in it. Old John stumbled along over the stones, cropping the grass as he went. Dorothy tugged at his halter and urged him on to the head of the lane where two farm-gates stood at right angles. One of them was open, and a number of horses were tethered in a row along the fence within. They whinneyed a cheerful greeting to John as Dorothy slipped his halter and shut him into the field adjoining. Now should she walk into temptation with her eyes and ears open? The gate stood wide, with only one field of perfumed meadow-grass between her and the lights and music of Slocum's barn ! The sound

of revelry by night could hardly have taken a more
innocent form than this rustic dancing of neighbors after a " raisin' bee," but had it been the rout
of Comus and his crew, and Dorothy the Lady
Una, trembling near, her heart could hardly have
throbbed more thickly as she crossed the dewy
meadow. A young maple stood within ten rods of
the barn, and here she crouched in shadow.

The great doors stood wide open, and lanterns
were hung from the beams lighting the space between the mows, where a dance was set, with
youths and maidens in two long rows. The fiddlers sat on barrel-heads near the door ; a lantern
hanging just behind projected their shadows across
the square of light on the trodden space in front
where they executed a grotesque pantomime, keeping time to the music with spectral wavings and
noddings. The dancers were Dorothy's young
neighbors, whom she had known and yet not
known all her life, but they had the strangeness of
familiar faces seen suddenly in some fantastic
dream.

Surely that was Nancy Slocum, in the bright
pink gown, heading the line of girls, and that
was Luke Jordan's sunburnt profile leaning
from his place to pluck a straw from the mow behind him. They were marching now, and the
measured tramp of feet, keeping solid time to the
fiddles, set a strange tumult vibrating in Dorothy's
blood ; and now it stopped with a thrill as she
recognized that Evesham was there marching with

the young men, and that his peer was not among
them.   The perception of his difference came to
her with a vivid shock.   He was coming forward
now, with his light, firm step, formidable in evening dress, and with a smile of subtle triumph in
his eyes, to meet Nancy Slocum, in the bright pink
gown ; Dorothy felt she hated pink, of all the colors her faith had abjured.   She could see, in spite
of the obnoxious gown, that Nancy was very
pretty.   He was taking her first by the right hand,
then by the left, and turning her gayly about ;—
and now they were meeting again, for the fourth
or fifth time, in the centre of the barn, with all
eyes upon them, and the music lingered while
Nancy, holding out her pink petticoats, coyly
revolved around him.   Then began a mysterious
turning, and clasping of hands, and weaving of
Nancy's pink frock and Evesham's dark blue coat
and white breeches in and out of the line of figures, until they met at the door, and taking each
other by both hands, swept with a joyous measure
to the head of the barn.   Dorothy gave a little
choking sigh.

What a senseless whirl it was ! But she was
thrilling with a new and strange excitement, too
near the edge of pain to be long endured as a pleasure.   If this were the influence of dancing, she did
not wonder so much at her father's scruples,—and
yet it held her like a spell.

All hands were lifted now, making an arch,
through which Evesham, holding Nancy by the

hands, raced stooping and laughing. As they emerged at the door, he threw up his head to shake a brown lock back. He looked flushed, and boy-ishly gay, and his hazel eye searched the darkness with that subtle ray of triumph in it which had made Dorothy afraid. She drew back behind the tree and pressed her hot cheek to the cool, rough bark. She longed for the stillness of the starlit meadow, and the dim lane, with its faint perfumes and whispering leaves.

But now suddenly the music stopped, and the dance broke up in a tumult of voices. Dorothy stole backward in the shadow of the tree-trunk, till it joined the darkness of the meadow, and then fled,—stumbling along with blinded eyes, and the music still vibrating in her ears. There came a quick rush of footsteps behind her, swishing through the long grass. She did not look back, but quickened her pace, struggling to reach the gate. Evesham was there before her. He had swung the gate to and was leaning with his back against it, laughing and panting.

" I've caught you, Dorothy, you little deceiver ! You'll not get rid of me to-night with any of your tricks. I'm going to take you home to your mother, and tell her you were peeping at the danc-ing.''

" Mother knows I am here,'' said Dorothy. " I asked her !'' Her knees were trembling, and her heart almost choked her with its throbbing.

" I'm so glad you don't dance, Dorothy. This

is much nicer than the barn ; and the katydids are
better fiddlers than old Darby and his son. I'll
open the gate if you will put your hand in mine, so
I can be sure of you—you little runaway !''

" I will stay here all night, first !'' said Dorothy,
in a low quivering voice.

" As you choose. I shall be happy as long as
you are here.''

Dead silence, while the katydids seemed to keep
time to their heart-beats ; the fiddles began tuning
for another reel, and the horses tethered near
stretched out their necks with low inquiring whin-
neys.

" Dorothy,'' said Evesham, softly, leaning toward her and trying to see her face in the darkness, " are you angry with me ? Don't you think
you deserve a little punishment for the trick you
played me at the mill-head ?''

" It was thy fault for wetting me !'' Dorothy
was too excited and angry to cry, but she was as
miserable as she had ever been in her life before.
" I didn't *want* thee to stay. People who force
themselves where they are not wanted must take
what they get !''

" What did you say, Dorothy ?''

" I say I didn't want thee then. I do not want
thee now ! Thee may go back to thy fiddling and
dancing ! I'd rather have one of those dumb
brutes for company to-night than thee, Walter
Evesham !''

" Very well ! The reel has begun,'' said Evesham. "Fanny Jordan is waiting to dance it with me, or if she isn't she ought to be! Shall I open the gate for you?"

She passed out in silence, and the gate swung to with a heavy jar. She made good speed down the lane, and then waited outside the fence till her breath came more quietly.

"Is that thee, Dorothy?" Rachel's voice called from the porch. She came out to meet her, and they went along the walk together. "How damp thy forehead is, child! is the night so warm?" They sat down on the low steps, and Dorothy slid her arm under her mother's and laid her soft palm against the one less soft by twenty years of toil for others. "Thee's not been long, dear; was it as much as thee expected?"

"Mother, it was dreadful! I never wish to hear a fiddle again as long as I live!"

Rachel opened the way for Dorothy to speak further; she was not without some mild stirrings of curiosity on the subject herself; but Dorothy had no more to say.

They went into the house soon after, and as they separated for the night, Dorothy clung to her mother with a little nervous laugh.

"Mother, what is that text about Ephraim?"

"Ephraim is joined to idols?" Rachel suggested.

"Yes! Ephraim is joined to his idols!" said Dorothy, lifting her head. "Let him go!"

"Let him *alone*," corrected Rachel.

"Let him *alone!*" Dorothy repeated. "That is better yet."

"What's thee thinking of, dear?"

"Oh, I'm thinking about the dance in the barn."

"I'm glad thee looks at it in that light," said Rachel.

Dorothy knelt by her bed in the low chamber under the eaves, crying to herself that she was not the child of her mother any more.

She felt she had lost something, which, in truth, had never been hers. It was only the unconscious poise of her unawakened girlhood which had been stirred. She had mistaken it for that abiding peace which is not lost or won in a day.

Dorothy could not stifle the spring thrills in her blood any more than she could crush its color out of her cheek or brush the ripples out of her bright hair, but she longed for the cool grays and the still waters. She prayed that the "grave and beautiful damsel called Discretion" might take her by the hand and lead her to that "upper chamber, whose name is Peace." She lay awake, listening to the music from the barn, and waiting through breathless silences for it to begin again. She wondered if Fanny Jordan had grown any prettier since she had seen her as a half-grown girl; and then she despised herself for the thought. The katydids seemed to beat their wings upon her brain, and all the noises of the night, far and near, came to her strained senses, as if her silent chamber were a whispering gallery. The clock struck twelve, and in the silence that followed she missed the music ; but voices, talking and laughing, were coming down the lane. There was the clink of a horse's hoof on the stones ; now it was lost on the turf ; and now they were all trooping noisily past the house. She buried her head in her pillow, and tried to bury with it the consciousness that she was wondering if Evesham were there, laughing with the rest.

Yes, Evesham was there. He walked with Farmer Jordan, behind the young men and girls, and discussed with him, somewhat absently, the war news and the prices of grain.

As they passed the dark old house, spreading its wide roofs, like a hen gathering her chickens under her wing, he became suddenly silent. A white curtain flapped in and out of an upper window. It was the window of the boys' room ; but Evesham's instincts failed him there.

"Queer kinks them old Friend preachers git into their heads sometimes !" said farmer Jordan, as they passed the empty mill. "Now what do you s'pose took Uncle Tommy Barton off right on top of plantin', leavin' his wife 'n' critters 'n' child'en to look after themselves ? Mighty good preachin' it ought to be, to make up for such practicin'. Wonderful set ag'in the war, Uncle Tommy is ! He's a-preachin' up peace now. But Lord ! all the preachin' sence Moses won't keep

men from fightin' when their blood's up and there's
ter'tory in it !''

" It makes saints of the women,'' said Evesham
shortly.

" Wal, yes ! Saints in heaven before their time,
some of 'em. There's Dorothy, now. *She'll* hoe
her row with any saint *in* the kingdom or out of it.
I never see a hulsomer-lookin' gal. My Luke, he
run the furrers in her corn-patch last May. Said
it made him sick to see a gal like that a-staggerin'
after a plow. She wouldn't more'n *half let* him !
She's a proud little piece. They're all proud,
Quakers is. I never could see no ' poorness of
spirit,' come to git at 'em ! And they're wonderful clannish, too. My Luke, he'd a notion he'd
like to run the hull concern—Dorothy 'n' all ; but
I told him he might 's well p'int off. Them
Quaker gals don't never marry out o' meetin'.
Besides, the farm's too poor !''

" Good-night, Mr. Jordan !'' said Evesham suddenly. " I'm off across lots !'' He leaped the
fence, crashed through the alder hedge-row, and
disappeared in the dusky meadow.

Evesham was by no means satisfied with his experiments in planetary distances. Somewhere, he
felt sure, either in his orbit or hers, there must be
a point where Dorothy would be less insensible to
the attraction of atoms in the mass. Thus far, she
had reversed the laws of the spheres, and the
greater had followed the less. When she had first
begun to hold a permanent place in his thoughts,

he had invested her with something of that atmosphere of peace and cool passivity which hedges in the women of her faith. It had been like a thin, clear glass; revealing her loveliness, but cutting off the magnetic currents. A young man is not long satisfied with the mystery his thoughts have woven around the woman who is their object. Evesham had grown impatient ; he had broken the spell of her sweet remoteness. He had touched her, and found her human,—deliciously, distractingly human, but with a streak of obduracy which history has attributed to the Quakers under persecution. In vain he haunted the mill-dam, and bribed the boys with traps and pop-guns, and lingered at the well-curb to ask Dorothy for water, which did not reach his thirst. She was there in the flesh, with her arms aloft, balancing the well-sweep, while he stooped with his lips at the bucket ; but in spirit she was unapproachable. He felt, with disgust at his own persistence, that she even grudged him the water ! He grew savage and restless, and fretted over the subtle changes which he counted in Dorothy, as the summer waned. She was thinner and paler,—perhaps with the heats of harvest, which had not, indeed, been burdensome from its abundance. Her eyes were darker and shyer, and her voice more languid. Was she wearing down, with all this work and care ? A fierce disgust possessed him, that this sweet life should be cast into the breach between faith and works.

He did not see that Rachel Barton had changed,

too,—with a change that meant more, at her age,
than Dorothy's flushings and palings.   He did not
miss the mother's bent form from the garden, or
the bench by the kitchen door, where she had been
used to wash the milk-things.

Dorothy washed the milk-things now, and the
mother spent her days in the sunny east room, between her bed and the easy-chair, where she sat
and mused for hours over the five letters she had
received from her husband in as many months.
The boys had, in a measure, justified their father's
faith in them, since Rachel's illness, and Dorothy
was released from much of her out-door work ; but
the silence of the kitchen, when she was there alone
with her ironing and dish-washing, was a heavier
burden than she had yet known.

Nature sometimes strikes in upon the hopeless
monotony of life in remote farm-houses, with one
of her phenomenal moods.   They come like besoms
of destruction ; but they scatter the web of stifling
routine ; they fling into the stiffening pool the
stone which jars the atoms into crystal.

The storms which had ambushed in the lurid
August skies, and circled ominously round the
horizon during the first weeks of September, broke
at last in an equinoctial which was long remembered in the mill-house.   It took its place in the
family calendar of momentous dates with the hard
winter of 1800 ; with the late frost, which coated
the incipient apples with ice, and froze the new

potatoes in the ground ; and with the year the typhus got into the valley.

The rain had been falling a night and a day. It had been welcomed with thanksgiving ; but it had worn out its welcome some hours since, and now the early darkness was coming on without a lull in the storm. Dorothy and the two biggest boys had made the rounds of the farm-buildings, seeing all safe for the second night. The barns and mill stood on high ground, while the house occupied the sheltered hollow between. Little streams from the hills were washing in turbid currents across the lower levels ; the waste-weir roared as in early spring ; the garden was inundated, and the meadow a shallow pond. The sheep had been driven into the upper barn floor ; the chickens were in the corn-bin ; and old John and the cows had been transferred from the stable, which stood low, to the weighing-floor of the mill. A gloomy echoing and gurgling sounded from the dark wheel-chamber, where the water was rushing under the wheel, and jarring it with its tumult. At eight o'clock the wood-shed was flooded, and water began to creep under the kitchen door. Dorothy and the boys carried armfuls of wood, and stacked them in the passage to the sitting-room, two steps higher up. At nine o'clock the boys were sent, protesting, to bed ; and Dorothy, looking out of their window, as she fumbled about in the dark for a pair of Shep's trowsers which needed mending, saw a lantern flickering up the road. It was Evesham, on

his way to the mill-dams.   The light glimmered on
his oil-skin coat as he climbed   the stile behind the
well-curb.

"He raised the flood-gates at noon," Dorothy
said to herself.   "I wonder if he is anxious about
the dams."   She resolved to watch for his return,
but she was busy settling her mother for the night
when she heard his footsteps on the porch.   The
roar of water from the hills startled Dorothy as she
opened the door ;—it had increased in violence
within an hour.   A gust of wind and rain followed
Evesham into the entry.

"Come in," she said, running lightly across the
sitting-room to close the door of her mother's
room.

He stood opposite her on the hearth-rug and
looked into her eyes across the estrangement of the
summer.   It was not Dorothy of the mill-head, or
of Slocum's meadow, or the cold maid of the well :
it was a very anxious, lovely little girl, in a crum-
bling old house, with a foot of water in the cellar,
and a sick mother in the next room.   She had forgotten about Ephraim and his idols ; she picked
up Shep's trowsers from the rug, where she had
dropped them, and looking intently at her thimble
finger, told him she was very glad he had come.

"Did you think I wouldn't come ?" said he.
"I'm going to take you home with me, Dorothy,—
you and your mother and the boys.   It's not fit for
you to be here alone !"

"Do you know of any danger ?"

"I *know* of none, but water's a thing you can't depend on. It's an ugly rain ; older men than your father remember nothing like it."

"I shall be glad to have mother go, and Jimmy ; —the house is very damp. It's an awful night for her to be out, though !"

"She *must* go !" said Evesham. "You must all go. I'll be back in half an hour—"

"*I* shall not go," Dorothy said ; "the boys and I must stay and look after the stock."

"What's that ?" Evesham was listening to a trickling of water outside the door.

"Oh ! it's from the kitchen ! The door's blown open, I guess !"

Dorothy looked out into the passage ; a strong wind was blowing in from the kitchen, where the water covered the floor and washed against the chimney.

"This is a nice state of things ! What's all this wood here for ?"

"The wood-shed's under water, you know."

"You must get yourself ready, Dorothy ! I'll come for your mother first in the chaise."

"I cannot go," she said ; "I don't believe there is any danger. This old house has stood for eighty years ; it's not likely this is the first big rain in all that time." Dorothy's spirits had risen. "Besides, I have a family of orphans to take care of ! See here," she said, stooping over a basket in the shadow of the chimney. It was the "hospital tent," and as she uncovered it, a brood of belated chickens stretched out their thin necks with plaintive peeps.

Dorothy covered them with her hands, and they nestled with cozy twitterings into silence.

"You're a kind of special providence, aren't you, Dorothy? But I've no sympathy with chickens who *will* be born just in time for the equinoctial."

"*I* didn't want them," said Dorothy, anxious to defend her management. "The old hen stole her nest, and she left them the day before the rain. She's making herself comfortable now in the corn-bin."

"She ought to be made an example of ;—that's the way of the world, however ;—retribution don't fall always on the right shoulders. I must go now. We'll take your mother and Jimmy first, and then, if you *won't* come, you shall let me stay with you. The mill is safe enough, anyhow."

Evesham returned with the chaise and a man who he insisted should drive away old John and the cows, so Dorothy should have less care. The mother was packed into the chaise with a vast collection of wraps, which almost obliterated Jimmy. As they started, Dorothy ran out in the rain with her mother's spectacles and the five letters, which always lay in a box on the table by her bed. Evesham took her gently by the arms and lifted her back across the puddles to the stoop.

As the chaise drove off, she went back to the sitting-room and crouched on the rug, her wet hair shining in the firelight. She took out her chickens one by one and held them under her chin, with tender words and finger-touches. If September chickens have hearts as susceptible as their bodies, Dorothy's orphans must have been imperilled by her caresses.

"Look here, Dorothy! Where's my trowsers?" cried Shep, opening the door at the foot of the stairs.

Reuby was behind him, fully arrayed in the aforesaid articles, and carrying the bedroom candle.

"Here they are—with a needle in them," said Dorothy. "What are you getting up in the middle of the night for?"

"Well, I guess it's time somebody's up. Who's that man driving off our cows?"

"Goosey! It's Walter Evesham's man. He came for mother and all of us, and he's taken old John and the cows to save us so much foddering."

"Ain't we going too?"

"I don't see why we should, just because there happens to be a little water in the kitchen. I've often seen it come in there before."

"Well, thee never saw anything like *this* before —nor anybody else, either," said Shep.

"I don't care," said Reuby; "I wish there'd come a reg'lar flood. We could climb up in the mill-loft and go sailin' down over Jordan's meadows. Wouldn't Luke Jordan open that big mouth of his to see us heave in sight about cock-crow—

three sheets in the wind, and the old tackle a-swingin' !''

" Do hush !'' said Dorothy. " We may have to try it yet.''

" There's an awful roarin' from our window,'' said Shep. " Thee can't half hear it down here. Come out on the stoop. The old ponds have got their dander up this time.''

They opened the door and listened, standing together on the low step. There was, indeed, a hoarse murmur from the hills which grew louder as they listened.

" Now she's comin' ! There goes the stable-door ! There was only one hinge left, anyway,'' said Reuby. " Mighty ! Look at that wave !''

It crashed through the gate, swept across the garden, and broke at their feet, sending a thin sheet of water over the floor and stoop.

" Now it's gone into the entry. Why didn't thee shut the door, Shep ?''

" Well, I think we'd better clear out, anyhow. Let's go over to the mill. Say, Dorothy, sha'n't we?''

" Wait. There comes another wave !''

The second onset was not so violent, but they hastened to gather together a few blankets, and the boys filled their pockets, with a delightful sense of unusualness and peril, almost equal to a ship-wreck or an attack by Indians. Dorothy took her unlucky chickens under her cloak and they made a rush, all together, across the road and up the slope to the mill.

" Why didn't we think to bring a lantern ?" said Dorothy, as they huddled together on the platform of the scale. " Will *thee* go back after one, Shep ?"

" If Reuby'll go, too."

" Well, *my* legs are wet enough now ! What's the use of a lantern ? Mighty Moses ! What's that ?"

" The old mill's got under weigh !" cried Shep. "*She's* going to tune up for Kingdom Come !"

A furious head of water was rushing along the race. The great wheel creaked and swung over, and with a shudder the old mill awoke from its long sleep. The cogs clenched their teeth, the shafting shook and rattled, the stones whirled merrily round.

" Now she goes it !" cried Shep, as the humming increased to a tremor, and the tremor to a wild, unsteady din, till the timbers shook and the bolts and windows rattled. " I just wish *father* could hear them old stones hum."

" Oh, this is awful !" said Dorothy. She was shivering, and sick with terror at this unseemly midnight revelry of her grandfather's old mill. It was as if it had awakened in a fit of delirium, and given itself up to a wild travesty of its years of peaceful work.

Shep was creeping about in the darkness.

" Look here ! We've got to stop this clatter somehow. The stones are hot now. The whole thing'll burn up like tinder if we can't chock her wheels."

" Shep ! Does thee *mean* it ?"

"Thee'll see if I don't. Thee won't need any lantern either."

"Can't we break away the race?"

"Oh, there's a way to stop it. There's the tip-trough, but it's down-stairs, and we can't reach the pole."

"I'll go," said Dorothy.

"It's outside, thee knows. Thee'll get awful *wet*, Dorothy."

"Well, I'd just as soon be drowned as burned up. Come with me to the head of the stairs."

They felt their way hand in hand in the darkness, and Dorothy went down alone. She had forgotten about the "tip-trough," but she understood its significance. In a few moments a cascade shot out over the wheel, sending the water far into the garden.

"Right over my chrysanthemum bed!" sighed Dorothy.

The wheel swung slower and slower, the mocking tumult subsided, and the old mill sank into sleep again.

There was nothing now to drown the roaring of the floods and the steady drive of the storm.

"There's a lantern," Shep called from the door. He had opened the upper half, and was shielding himself behind it. "I guess it's Evesham coming back for us. He's a pretty good sort of a fellow, after all; don't thee think so, Dorothy? He owes us something for drowning us out at the sheep-washing."

"What *does all* this mean?" said Dorothy, as Evesham swung himself over the half-door, and his lantern showed them in their various phases of wetness.

"There's a big leak in the lower dam! I've been afraid of it all along; there's something wrong in the principle of the thing."

Dorothy felt as if he had called her grandfather a fraud, and her father a delusion and a snare. She had grown up in the belief that the mill-dams were part of Nature's original plan, in laying the foundations of the hills;—but it was no time to be resentful, and the facts were against her.

"Dorothy," said Evesham, as he tucked the buffalo about her, "this is the second time I've tried to save you from drowning, but you never will wait! *I'm* all ready to be a hero, but *you* won't be a heroine."

"I'm too practical for a heroine," said Dorothy. "There! I've forgotten my chickens."

"I'm glad of it! Those chickens were a mistake. They oughtn't to be perpetuated."

Youth and happiness can stand a great deal of cold water; but it was not to be expected that Rachel Barton should be especially benefited by her night journey through the floods. Evesham waited in the hall when he heard the door of her room open next morning. Dorothy came slowly down the stairs; he knew by her lingering step and the softly closed door that she was not happy.

"Mother is very sick," she answered his inquiry.

"It is like the turn of inflammation and rheuma-
tism she had once before.   It will be very slow, —
and oh ! it is such suffering !   Why *do* the best
women in the world have to suffer so ?"

"Will you let me talk things over with you after
breakfast, Dorothy ?"

"Oh yes !" she said ;   "there is so much to do
and think about.   I *wish* father *would* come home !"

The tears came into Dorothy's eyes as she looked
at him.   Rest—such as she had never known, or
felt the need of till now—and strength immeasur-
able, since it would multiply her own by an unknown quantity, stood within reach of her hand,
but she might not put it out !   And Evesham was
dizzy with the struggle between longing and resolution.

He had braced his nerves for a long and hungry
waiting, but fate had yielded suddenly ;—the
floods had brought her to him,—his flotsam and
jetsam, more precious than all the guarded treas-
ures of the earth.   She had come, with all her girl-
ish, unconscious beguilements, and all her womanly
cares, and anxieties too.   He must strive against her
sweetness, while he helped her to bear her burdens.

"Now about the boys, Dorothy," he said two
hours later, as they stood together by the fire in
the low, oak-finished room at the foot of the stairs,
which was his office and book-room.   The door
was ajar, so Dorothy might hear her mother's bell.
"Don't you think they had better be sent to school
somewhere ?"

"Yes," said Dorothy, "they *ought* to go to school—but—well, I may as well tell thee the truth! There's very little to do it with. We've had a poor summer. I suppose I've managed badly, and mother has been sick a good while."

"You've forgotten about the pond-rent, Dorothy."

"No," she said, with a quick flush; "I hadn't forgotten it; but I couldn't *ask* thee for it!"

"I spoke to your father about monthly payments; but he said better leave it to accumulate for emergencies. Shouldn't you call this an 'emergency,' Dorothy?"

"But does thee think we ought to ask rent for a pond that has all leaked away?"

"Oh, there's pond enough left, and I've used it a dozen times over this summer! I would be ashamed to tell you, Dorothy, how my horn has been exalted in your father's absence. However, retribution has overtaken me at last; I'm responsible, you know, for all the damage last night. It was in the agreement that I should keep up the dams."

"Oh!" said Dorothy; "is thee sure?"

Evesham laughed.

"If your father were like any other man, Dorothy, he'd make me 'sure,' when he gets home! I will defend myself to this extent: I've patched and propped them all summer, after every rain, and tried to provide for the fall storms; but there's a flaw in the original plan—"

"Thee said that once before," said Dorothy. "I wish thee wouldn't say it again."

"Why not ?"

"Because I love those old mill-dams ! I've trot· ted over them ever since I could walk alone !"

"You shall trot over them still ! We will make them as strong as the everlasting hills. They shall outlast our time, Dorothy."

"Well, about the rent," said Dorothy. "I'm afraid it will not take us through the winter, unless there is something I can do. Mother couldn't possibly be moved now, and if she could, it will be months before the house is fit to live in. But we cannot stay here in comfort, unless thy mother will let me make up in some way. Mother will not need me all the time, and I know thy mother hires women to spin."

"She'll let you do all you like, if it will make you any happier. But you don't know how much money is coming to you. Come, let us look over the figures."

He lowered the lid of the black mahogany secretary, placed a chair for Dorothy, and opened a great ledger before her, bending down, with one hand on the back of the chair, the other turning the leaves of the ledger. Considering the index, and the position of the letter B in the alphabet, he was a long time finding his place. Dorothy looked out of the window, over the tops of the yellowing woods, to the gray and turbid river below. Where the hemlocks darkened the channel of the glen, she

heard the angry floods rushing down. The form-
less rain mists hung low, and hid the opposite
shore.

"See!" said Evesham, with his finger wandering rather vaguely down the page. "Your father
went away on the third of May. The first month's
rent came due on the third of June. That was the
day I opened the gate and let the water down on
you, Dorothy. I'm responsible for everything, you
see,—even for the old ewe that was drowned!"

His words came in a dream as he bent over her,
resting his unsteady hand heavily on the ledger.

Dorothy laid her cheek on the date she could not
see, and burst into tears.

"Don't—please don't!" he said, straightening
himself, and locking his hands behind him. "I
am human, Dorothy!"

The weeks of Rachel's sickness that followed
were perhaps the best discipline Evesham's life had
ever known. He held the perfect flower of his
bliss, unclosing in his hand ; yet he might barely
permit himself to breathe its fragrance! His
mother had been a strong and prosperous woman ;
there was little he could ever do for her. It was
well for him to feel the weight of helpless infirmity
in his arms, as he lifted Dorothy's mother from
side to side of her bed, while Dorothy's hands
smoothed the coverings. It was well for him to
see the patient endurance of suffering, such as his
youth and strength defied. It was bliss to wait on
Dorothy, and follow her with little watchful hom-

ages, received with a shy wonder which was delicious to him,—for Dorothy's nineteen years had
been too full of service to others to leave much
room for dreams of a kingdom of her own.   Her
silent presence in her mother's sick-room awed
him.   Her gentle, decisive voice and ways, her
composure and unshaken endurance through nights
of watching and days of anxious confinement and
toil, gave him a new reverence for the mysteries of
her unfathomable womanhood.

The time of Friend Barton's return drew near.
It must be confessed that Dorothy welcomed it
with a little dread, and Evesham did not welcome
it at all.   On the contrary, the thought of it
roused all his latent obstinacy and aggressiveness.
The first day or two after the momentous arrival
wore a good deal upon every member of the family,
except Margaret Evesham, who was provided with
a philosophy of her own, which amounted almost
to a gentle obtuseness, and made her a comfortable
non-conductor, preventing more electric souls from
shocking each other.

On the morning of the fourth day, Dorothy
came out of her mother's room with a tray of
empty dishes in her hands.   She saw Evesham at
the stair-head and hovered about in the shadowy
part of the hall till he should go down.

"Dorothy," he said, "I'm waiting for you."
He took the tray from her and rested it on the
banisters.   "Your father and I have talked over
all the business.   He's got the impression I'm one

of the most generous fellows in the world. I intend to let him rest in that delusion for the present. Now may I speak to him about something
else, Dorothy? Have I not waited long enough
for my heart's desire?"

"Take care!" said Dorothy, softly,—"thee'll
upset the tea-cups!"

"Confound the tea-cups!" He stooped to place
the irrelevant tray on the floor, but now Dorothy
was half-way down the staircase. He caught her
on the landing, and taking both her hands, drew
her down on the step beside him.

"Dorothy, this is the second time you've taken
advantage of my unsuspicious nature! This time
you shall be punished! You needn't try to hide
your face, you little traitor! There's no repentance in you!"

"If I'm to be punished there's no need of repentance."

"Dorothy, do you know, I've never heard you
speak my name, except once, when you were angry
with me."

"When was that?"

"The night I caught you at the gate. You said,
'I would rather have one of those dumb brutes for
company than thee, Walter Evesham.' You said
it in the fiercest little voice! Even the 'thee'
sounded as if you hated me."

"I did," said Dorothy promptly. "I had reason to."

"Do you hate me now, Dorothy?"

" Not so much as I did then."

" What an implacable little Quaker you are !"

" A tyrant is *always* hated," said Dorothy, trying to release her hands.

" If you will look in my eyes, Dorothy, and call me by my name, just once,—I'll let ' thee ' go."

" Walter Evesham !" said Dorothy, with great firmness and decision.

" No ! that won't do ! You must look at me,—and say it softly,—in a little sentence, Dorothy !"

" Will thee please let me go, Walter ?"

Walter Evesham was a man of his word, but as Dorothy sped away, he looked as if he wished he were not.

The next evening, Friend Barton sat by his wife's easy-chair, drawn into the circle of firelight, with his elbows on his knees, and his head between his hands.

The worn spot on the top of his head had widened considerably during the summer, but Rachel looked stronger and brighter than she had for many a day.   There was even a little flush on her cheek, but that might have come from the excitement of a long talk with her husband.

" I'm sorry thee takes it so hard, Thomas ; I was afraid thee would.   But the way didn't seem to open for me to do much.   I can see now, that Dorothy's inclinations have been turning this way for some time, though it's not likely she would own it, poor child ; and Walter Evesham's not one who is easily gainsayed.   If *thee* could only feel

differently about it, I can't say but it would make
me very happy to see Dorothy's heart satisfied.
Can't thee bring thyself into unity with it, father?
He's a nice young man. They're nice folks. Thee
can't complain of the *blood.* Margaret Evesham
tells me a cousin of hers married one of the Law-
rences, so we are kind of kin, after all.''

" I don't complain of the blood ; they're well
enough placed as far as the world is concerned !
But their ways are not our ways, Rachel ! Their
faith is not our faith !''

" Well ! I can't see such a very great difference,
come to live among them ! ' By their fruits ye
shall know them.' To comfort the widow and the
fatherless, and keep ourselves unspotted from the
world !—thee's always preached that, father ! I
really can't see any more worldliness here than
among many households with us,—and I'm sure if
we haven't been the widow and the fatherless this
summer, we've been next to it !''

Friend Barton raised his head a little, and rested
his forehead on his clasped hands.

" Rachel,'' he said, " look at that !'' He pointed
upward to an ancient sword with belt and trap-
pings, which gleamed on the panelled chimney-
piece—crossed by an old queen's arm. Evesham
had given up his large sunny room to Dorothy's
mother, but he had not removed all his lares and
penates.

" Yes, dear ; that's his grandfather's sword—
Colonel Evesham, who was killed at Saratoga !''

"Why does he hang up that thing of abomination for a light and a guide to his footsteps, if his way be not far from ours ?"

"Why, father! Colonel Evesham was a good man !—I dare say he fought for the same reason that thee preaches—because he felt it his duty !"

"I find no fault with *him*, Rachel. Doubtless he followed his light, as thee says ; but he followed it in better ways too. He cleared land and built a homestead and a meeting-house. Why don't his grandson hang up his old broad-ax and plough-share, and worship *them*, if he must have idols, instead of that symbol of strife and bloodshed. Does thee want our Dorothy's children to grow up under the shadow of that sword ?"

There was a stern light of prophecy in the old man's eyes.

"Maybe Walter Evesham would take it down," said Rachel, leaning back wearily and closing her eyes. "I never was much of a hand to argue, even if I had the strength for it ; but it would hurt me a good deal—I must say it—if thee denies Dorothy in this matter, Thomas. It's a very serious thing to have old folks try to turn young hearts the way they think they ought to go. I remember now,—I was thinking about it last night, and it all came back as fresh ! I don't know that I ever told thee about that young friend who visited me before I heard thee preach at Stony Valley ? Well ! *father*, *he* was wonderful pleased with him, but I didn't feel any drawing that way.

He urged me a good deal, more than was pleasant for either of us. He wasn't at all reconciled to thee, Thomas, if thee remember.''

" I remember," said Thomas Barton, " it was an anxious time.''

" Well dear, if father *had* insisted, and sent thee away, I can't say but life would have been a very different thing to me.''

" I thank thee for saying it, Rachel." Friend Barton's head drooped between his hands.

" Thee's suffered much through me ; thee's had a hard life, but thee's been well beloved.''

The flames leaped and flickered in the chimney, they touched the wrinkled hands, whose only beauty was in their deeds ; they crossed the room and lit the pillows where, for three generations, young heads had dreamed, and gray heads had watched and suffered ; then they mounted to the chimney and struck a gleam from the sword.

" Well, father," said Rachel, " what answer is thee going to give Walter Evesham ?''

" I shall say no more, my dear. Let the young folks have their way. There's strife and contention enough in the world without my stirring up more. And it may be I'm resisting the Master's will ; I left her in His care : this may be His way of dealing with her.''

Walter Evesham did not take down his grandfather's sword. Fifty years later another went up beside it,—the sword of a young Evesham who never left the field of Shiloh ; and beneath them both hangs the portrait of the Quaker grandmother, Dorothy Evesham, at the age of sixty-nine.

The golden ripples, silver now, are hidden under a "round-eared cap," the quick flush has faded in her cheek, and fold upon fold of snowy gauze and creamy silk are crossed over the bosom that thrilled to the fiddles of Slocum's barn. She has found the cool grays and the still waters ; but on Dorothy's children rests the "Shadow of the Sword " !

AN INSPIRED LOBBYIST.

By J. W. DeForest.

A CERTAIN fallen angel (politeness toward his numerous and influential friends forbids me to mention his name abruptly) lately entered into the body of Mr. Ananias Pullwool, of Washington, D. C.

As the said body was a capacious one, having been greatly enlarged circumferentially since it acquired its full longitude, there was accommodation in it for both the soul of Pullwool himself (it was a very little one) and for his distinguished visitant. Indeed, there was so much room in it that they never crowded each other, and that Pullwool hardly knew, if he even so much as mistrusted, that there was a chap in with him. But other people must have been aware of this double tenantry, or at least must have been shrewdly suspicious of it, for it soon became quite common to hear fellows say, " Pullwool has got the Devil in him."

. Atlantic Monthly, December, 1872.

There was, indeed, a remarkable change — a
change not so much moral as physical and mental
—in this gentleman's ways of deporting and be-
having himself. From being logy in movement
and slow if not absolutely dull in mind, he became
wonderfully agile and energetic. He had been a
lobbyist, and he remained a lobbyist still, but such
a different one, so much more vigorous, eager,
clever, and impudent, that his best friends (if he
could be said to have any friends) scarcely knew
him for the same Pullwool. His fat fingers were
in the buttonholes of Congressmen from the time
when they put those buttonholes on in the morning to the time when they took them off at night.
He seemed to be at one and the same moment
treating some honorable member in the bar-room
of the Arlington and running another honorable
member to cover in the committee-rooms of the
Capitol. He log-rolled bills which nobody else
believed could be log-rolled, and he pocketed fees
which absolutely and point-blank refused to go into
other people's pockets. During this short period
of his life he was the most successful and famous
lobbyist in Washington, and the most sought after
by the most rascally and desperate claimants of
unlawful millions.

But, like many another man who has the Devil
in him, Mr. Pullwool ran his luck until he ran
himself into trouble. An investigating committee
pounced upon him ; he was put in confinement for
refusing to answer questions ; his filchings were

held up to the execration of the envious both by
virtuous members and a virtuous press ; and when
he at last got out of durance he found it good to
quit the District of Columbia for a season. Thus
it happened that Mr. Pullwool and his eminent
lodger took the cars and went to and fro upon the
earth seeking what they might devour.

In the course of their travels they arrived in a
little State, which may have been Rhode Island,
or may have been Connecticut, or may have been
one of the Pleiades, but which at all events had
two capitals. Without regard to Morse's Gazetteer, or to whatever other Gazetteer may now be
in currency, we shall affirm that one of these capitals was called Slowburg and the other Fastburg.
For some hundreds of years (let us say five hundred,
in order to be sure and get it high enough) Slowburg and Fastburg had shared between them, turn
and turn about, year on and year off, all the gu-
bernatorial and legislative pomps and emoluments
that the said State had to bestow. On the 1st of
April of every odd year the governor, preceded
by citizen soldiers, straddling or curvetting
through the mud — the governor, followed by
twenty barouches full of eminent citizens, who
were not known to be eminent at any other time,
but who made a rush for a ride on this occasion as
certain old ladies do at funerals—the governor,
taking off his hat to pavements full of citizens of
all ages, sizes, and colors, who did not pretend to
be eminent—the governor, catching a fresh cold at

every corner, and wishing the whole thing were
passing at the equator,—the governor triumphantly entered Slowburg, — observe, Slowburg,—
read his always enormously long message there,
and convened the legislature there.   On the 1st of
April of every even year the same governor, or a
better one who had succeeded him, went through
the same ceremonies in Fastburg.   Each of these
capitals boasted, or rather blushed over, a shabby
old barn of a State-House, and each of them main-
tained a company of foot-guards and ditto of
horse-guards, the latter very loose in their saddles.
In each the hotels and boarding-houses had a full
year and a lean year, according as the legislature
sat in the one or in the other.   In each there was
a loud call for fresh shad and stewed oysters, or a
comparatively feeble call for fresh shad and stewed
oysters, under the same biennial conditions.

Such was the oscillation of grandeur and power
between the two cities.   It was an old-time arrangement, and like many other old-fashioned
things, as for instance wood fires in open fire-
places, it had not only its substantial merits but its
superficial inconveniences.   Every year certain ancient officials were obliged to pack up hundreds of
public documents and expedite them from Fastburg
to Slowburg, or from Slowburg back to Fastburg.
Every year there was an expense of a few dollars
on this account, which the State treasurer figured
up with agonies of terror, and which the opposition roared at as if the administration could have

helped it. The State-Houses were two mere de-
formities of patched plaster and leprous whitewash ;
they were such shapeless, graceless, dilapidated
wigwams, that no sensitive patriot could look at
them without wanting to fly to the uttermost parts
of the earth ; and yet it was not possible to build
new ones, and hardly possible to obtain appropriations enough to shingle out the weather ; for
Fastburg would vote no money to adorn Slowburg, and Slowburg was equally niggardly toward
Fastburg. The same jealousy produced the same
frugality in the management of other public insti-
tutions, so that the patients of the lunatic asylum
were not much better lodged and fed than the
average sane citizen, and the gallows-birds in the
State's prison were brought down to a temperance
which caused admirers of that species of fowl to
tremble with indignation. In short, the two capitals were as much at odds as the two poles of a
magnet, and the results of this repulsion were not
all of them worthy of hysterical admiration.

But advantages seesawed with disadvantages.
In this double-ender of a State political jobbery
was at fault, because it had no headquarters. It
could not get together a ring ; it could not raise a
corps of lobbyists. Such few axe-grinders as there
were had to dodge back and forth between the
Fastburg grindstone and the Slowburg grindstone,
without ever fairly getting their tools sharpened.
Legislature here and legislature there ; it was like
guessing at a pea between two thimbles ; you could

hardly ever put your finger on the right one. Then what one capital favored the other disfavored ; and between them appropriations were kicked and hustled under the table ; the grandest of railroad schemes shrunk into waste-paper baskets ; in short, the public treasury was next door to the unapproachable. Such, indeed, was the desperate condition of lobbyists in this State, that, had it contained a single philanthropist of the advanced radical stripe, he would surely have brought in a bill for their relief and encouragement.

Into the midst of this happily divided community dropped Mr. Ananias Pullwool with the Devil in him. It remains to be seen whether this pair could figure up anything worth pocketing out of the problem of two capitals.

It was one of the even years, and the legislature met in Fastburg, and the little city was brimful. Mr. Pullwool with difficulty found a place for himself without causing the population to slop over. Of course he went to a hotel, for he needed to make as many acquaintances as possible, and he knew that a bar was a perfect hot-house for ripening such friendships as he cared for. He took the best room he could get ; and as soon as chance favored he took a better one, with parlor attached ; and on the sideboard in the parlor he always had cigars and decanters. The result was that in a week or so he was on jovial terms with several senators, numerous members of the lower house, and all the members of the " third house." But lobbying did

not work in Fastburg as Mr. Pullwool had found it
to work in other capitals. He exhibited the most
dazzling double-edged axes, but nobody would
grind them ; he pointed out the most attractive
and convenient of logs for rolling, but nobody
would put a lever to them.

" What the doose does this mean ?" he at last inquired of Mr. Josiah Dicker, a member who had
smoked dozens of his cigars and drunk quarts out
of his decanters. " I don't understand this little
old legislature at all, Mr. Dicker. Nobody wants
to make any money ; at least, nobody has the spirit
to try to make any. And yet the State is full ;
never been bled a drop ; full as a tick. What does
it mean ?"

Mr. Dicker looked disconsolate. Perhaps it may
be worth a moment's time to explain that he could
not well look otherwise. Broken in fortune and
broken in health, he was a failure and knew it.
His large forehead showed power, and he was
in fact a lawyer of some ability ; and still he
could not support his family, could not keep a
mould of mortgages from creeping all over his
house-lot, and had so many creditors that he could
not walk the streets comfortably. The trouble
lay in hard drinking, with its resultant waste of
time, infidelity to trust, and impatience of application. Thin, haggard, duskily pallid, deeply
wrinkled at forty, his black eyes watery and set in
baggy circles of a dull brown, his lean dark hands
shaky and dirty, his linen wrinkled and buttonless,

his clothing frayed and unbrushed, he was an impersonation of failure. He had gone into the legislature with a desperate hope of somehow finding money in it, and as yet he had discovered nothing more than his beggarly three dollars a day, and he felt himself more than ever a failure. No wonder that he wore an air of profound depression, approaching to absolute wretchedness and threatening suicide.

He looked the more cast down by contrast with the successful Mr. Pullwool, gaudily alight with satin and jewelry, and shining with conceit. Pullwool, by the way, although a dandy (that is, such a dandy as one sees in gambling-saloons and behind liquor-bars), was far from being a thing of beauty. He was so obnoxiously gross and shapeless, that it seemed as if he did it on purpose and to be irritating. His fat head was big enough to make a dwarf of, hunchback and all. His mottled cheeks were vast and pendulous to that degree that they inspired the imaginative beholder with terror, as reminding him of avalanches and landslides which might slip their hold at the slightest shock and plunge downward in a path of destruction. One puffy eyelid drooped in a sinister way ; obviously that was the eye that the Devil had selected for his own ; he kept it well curtained for purposes of concealment. Looking out of this peep-hole, the Satanic badger could see a short, thick nose, and by leaning forward a little he could get a glimpse of a broad chin of several stories. Another unpleasing feature was a

full set of false teeth, which grinned in a ravenous
fashion that was truly disquieting, as if they were
capable of devouring the whole internal revenue.
Finally, this continent of physiognomy was diver-
sified by a gigantic hairy wart, which sprouted
defiantly from the temple nearest the game eye, as
though Lucifer had accidentally poked one of his
horns through. Mr. Dicker, who was a sensitive,
squeamish man (as drunkards sometimes are,
through bad digestion and shaky nerves), could
hardly endure the sight of this wart, and always
wanted to ask Pullwool why he didn't cut it off.

"What's the meaning of it all?" persisted the
Washington wire-puller, surveying the Fastburg
wire-puller with bland superiority, much as the city
mouse may have surveyed the country mouse.

"Two capitals," responded Dicker, withdrawing
his nervous glance from the wart, and locking his
hands over one knee to quiet their trembling.

Mr. Pullwool, having the Old Harry in him, and
being consequently full of all malice and subtlety,
perceived at once the full scope and force of the
explanation.

"I see," he said, dropping gently back into his
arm-chair, with the plethoric, soft movement of a
subsiding pillow. The puckers of his cumbrous
eyelids drew a little closer together; his bilious
eyes peered out cautiously between them, like sal-
low assassins watching through curtained windows; for a minute or so he kept up what might
without hyperbole be called a devil of a thinking.

"I've got it," he broke out at last. "Dicker, I want you to bring in a bill to make Fastburg the only capital."

"What is the use?" asked the legislator, looking more disconsolate, more hopeless than ever. "Slowburg will oppose it and beat it."

"Never you mind," persisted Mr. Pullwool. "You bring in your little bill and stand up for it like a man. There's money in it. You don't see it? Well, I do; I'm used to seeing money in things; and in this case I see it plain. As sure as whiskey is whiskey, there's money in it."

Mr. Pullwool's usually dull and, so to speak, extinct countenance was fairly alight and aflame with exultation. It was almost a wonder that his tallowy person did not gutter beneath the blaze, like an over-fat candle under the flaring of a wick too large for it.

"Well, I'll bring in the bill," agreed Mr. Dicker, catching the enthusiasm of his counsellor and shaking off his lethargy. He perceived a dim promise of fees, and at the sight his load of despondency dropped away from him, as Christian's burden loosened in presence of the cross. He looked a little like the confident, resolute Tom Dicker, who twenty years before had graduated from college the brightest, bravest, most eloquent fellow in his class, and the one who seemed to have before him the finest future.

"Snacks!" said Mr. Pullwool.

At this brazen word Mr. Dicker's countenance

fell again ; he was ashamed to talk so frankly
about plundering his fellow-citizens ; "a little
grain of conscience turned him sour."

" I will take pay for whatever I can do as a
lawyer," he stammered.

" Get out !" laughed the Satanic one. " You
just take all there is a-going ! You need it bad
enough. I know when a man's hard up. I know
the signs. I've been as bad off as you ; had to
look all ways for five dollars ; had to play second
fiddle and say thanky. But what I offer you ain't
a second fiddle. It's as good a chance as my
own. Even divides. One half to you and one
half to me. You know the people and I know
the ropes. It's a fair bargain. What do you.
say ?"

Mr. Dicker thought of his decayed practice and
his unpaid bills ; and flipping overboard his little
grain of conscience, he said, " Snacks."

" All right," grinned Pullwool, his teeth gleaming alarmingly. " Word of a gentleman," he added,
extending his pulpy hand, loaded with ostentatious
rings, and grasping Dicker's recoiling fingers.
" Harness up your little bill as quick as you can,
and drive it like Jehu. Fastburg to be the only capital. Slowburg no claims at all, historical, geographical, or economic. The old arrangement a hum-
bug ; as inconvenient as a fifth wheel of a coach ;
costs the State thousands of greenbacks every year.
Figure it all up statistically and dab it over with
your shiniest rhetoric and make a big thing of it

every way. That's what you've got to do ; that's
your little biz. I'll tend to the rest."

" I don't quite see where the money is to come
from," observed Mr. Dicker.

" Leave that to me," said the veteran of the
lobbies ; " my name is Pullwool, and I know how
to pull the wool over men's eyes, and then I know
how to get at their britches-pockets. You bring in
your bill and make your speech. Will you do it ?"

" Yes," answered Dicker, bolting all scruples in
another half tumbler of brandy.

He kept his word. As promptly as parliamentary
forms and mysteries would allow, there was a bill
under the astonished noses of honorable lawgivers,
.removing the seat of legislation from Slowburg and
centring it in Fastburg. This bill Mr. Thomas
Dicker supported with that fluency and fiery enthusiasm of oratory which had for a time enabled him
to show as the foremost man of his State. Great
was the excitement, great the rejoicing and anger.
The press of Fastburg sent forth shrieks of exultation, and the press of Slowburg responded with
growlings of disgust. The two capitals and the two
geographical sections which they represented were
ready to fire Parrott guns at each other, without
regard to life and property in the adjoining regions
of the earth. If there was a citizen of the little Com-
monwealth who did not hear of this bill and did not
talk of it, it was because that citizen was as deaf
as a post and as dumb as an oyster. Ordinary
political distinctions were forgotten, and the old

party-whips could not manage their very wheel-horses, who went snorting and kicking over the traces in all directions. In short, both in the legislature and out of it, nothing was thought of but the question of the removal of the capital.

Among the loudest of the agitators was Mr. Pullwool ; not that he cared one straw whether the capital went to Fastburg, or to Slowburg, or to Ballyhack ; but for the money which he thought he saw in the agitation he did care mightily, and to get that money he labored with a zeal which was not of this world alone. At the table of his hotel, and in the barroom of the same institution, and in the lobbies of the legislative hall, and in editorial sanctums and barbers' shops, and all other nooks of gossip, he trumpeted the claims of Fastburg as if that little city were the New Jerusalem and deserved to be the metropolis of the sidereal universe. All sorts of trickeries, too ; he sent spurious telegrams and got fictitious items into the newspapers ; he lied through every medium known to the highest civilization. Great surely was his success, for the row which he raised was tremendous. But a row alone was not enough ; it was the mere breeze upon the surface of the waters ; the treasure-ship below was still to be drawn up and gutted.

" It will cost money," he whispered confidentially to capitalists and land-owners. " We must have the sinews of war, or we can't carry it on. There's your city lots goin' to double in value if this bill goes through. What per cent will you pay on the advance ? That's the question. Put your hands in your pockets and pull 'em out full, and put back ten times as much. It's a sure investment ; warranted to yield a hundred per cent ; the safest and biggest thing agoing."

Capitalists and land-owners and merchants hearkened and believed and subscribed. The slyest old hunks in Fastburg put a faltering forefinger into his long pocket-book, touched a greenback which had been laid away there as neatly as a corpse in its coffin, and resurrected it for the use of Mr. Pullwool. By tens, by twenties, by fifties, and by hundreds the dollars of the ambitious citizens of the little metropolis were charmed into the portemonnaie of this rattlesnake of a lobbyist.

" I never saw a greener set," chuckled Pullwool. " By jiminy, I believe they'd shell out for a bill to make their town a seaport, if it was a hundred miles from a drop of water."

But he was not content with individual subscriptions, and conscientiously scorned himself until he had got at the city treasury.

" The corporation must pony up," he insisted, with the mayor. " This bill is just shaking in the wind for lack of money. Fastburg must come down with the dust. You ought to see to it. What are you chief magistrate for ? Ain't it to tend to the welfare of the city ? Look here, now ; you call the common council together ; secret session, you understand. You call 'em together and let me talk

to 'em. I want to make the loons comprehend that
it's their duty to vote something handsome for this
measure.''

The mayor hummed and hawed one way, and
then he hawed and hummed the other way, and
the result was that he granted the request. There
was a secret session in the council-room, with his
honor at the top of the long green table, with a
row of more or less respectable functionaries on
either side of it, and with Mr. Pullwool and the
Devil at the bottom. Of course it is not to be
supposed that this last-named personage was visible
to the others, or that they had more than a vague
suspicion of his presence. Had he fully revealed
himself, had he plainly exhibited his horns and
hoofs, or even so much as uncorked his perfume-
bottle of brimstone, it is more than probable that
the city authorities would have been exceedingly
scandalized, and they might have adjourned the
session. As it was, seeing nothing more disagreeable than the obese form of the lobbyist, they listened calmly while he unfolded his project.

Mr. Pullwool spoke at length, and to Fastburg
ears eloquently. Fastburg must be the sole capital ;
it had every claim, historical, geographical, and
commercial, to that distinction ; it ought, could,
would, and should be the sole capital ; that was
about the substance of his exordium.

'' But, gentlemen, it will cost,'' he went on.
'' There is an unscrupulous and furious opposition
to the measure. The other side—those fellows from

Slowburg and vicinity—are putting their hands into their britches-pockets. You must put your hands into yours. The thing will be worth millions to Fastburg. But it will cost thousands. Are you ready to fork over? *Are* you ready?"

"What's the figure?" asked one of the councilmen. "What do you estimate?"

"Gentlemen, I shall astonish *some* of you," answered Mr. Pullwool, cunningly. It was well put; it was as much as to say, "I shall astonish the green ones; of course the really strong heads among you won't be in the least bothered." "I estimate," he continued, "that the city treasury will have to put up a good round sum, say a hundred thousand dollars, be it more or less."

A murmur of surprise, of chagrin, and of something like indignation ran along the line of official mustaches. "Nonsense," "The dickens," "Can't be done," "We can't think of it," broke out several councilmen, in a distinctly unparliamentary manner.

"Gentlemen, one moment," pleaded Pullwool, passing his greasy smile around the company, as though it were some kind of refreshment. "Look at the whole job; it's a big job. We must have lawyers; we must have newspapers in all parts of the State; we must have writers to work up the historical claims of the city; we must have fellows to buttonhole honorable members; we must have fees for honorable members themselves. How can you do it for less?"

Then he showed a schedule ; so much to this wire-puller and that and the other ; so much apiece to so many able editors ; so much for eminent legal counsel ; finally, a trifle for himself. And one hundred thousand dollars or thereabouts was what the schedule footed up, turn it whichever way you would.

Of course this common council of Fastburg did not dare to vote such a sum for such a purpose. Mr. Pullwool had not expected that it would ; all that he had hoped for was the half of it ; but that half he got.

"Did they do it ?" breathlessly inquired Tom Dicker of him, when he returned to the hotel.

"They done it," calmly, yet triumphantly, responded Mr. Pullwool.

"Thunder !" exclaimed the amazed Dicker. "You are the most extraordinary man ! You must have the very Devil in you !"

Instead of being startled by this alarming supposition, Mr. Pullwool looked gratified. People thus possessed generally do look gratified when the possession is alluded to.

But the inspired lobbyist did not pass his time in wearing an aspect of satisfaction. When there was money to get and to spend he could run his fat off almost as fast as if he were pouring it into candle-moulds. The ring—the famous capital ring of Fastburg—must be seen to, its fingers greased, and its energy quickened. Before he rolled his apple-dumpling of a figure into bed that night he had interviewed Smith and Brown the editors, Jones and Robinson the lawyers, Smooth and Slow the literary characters, various lobbyists, and various lawgivers.

" Work, gentlemen, and capitalize Fastburg and get your dividends," was his inspiring message to one and all. He promised Smith and Brown ten dollars for every editorial, and five dollars for every humbugging telegram, and two dollars for every telling item. Jones and Robinson were to have five hundred dollars apiece for concurrent legal statements of the claim of the city ; Smooth and Slow, as being merely authors and so not accustomed to obtain much for their labor, got a hundred dollars between them for working up the case historically. To the lobbyists and members Pullwool was munificent ; it seemed as if those gentlemen could not be paid enough for their " influence ;" as if they alone had that kind of time which is money. Only, while dealing liberally with them, the inspired one did not forget himself. A thousand for Mr. Sly ; yes, Mr. Sly was to receipt for a thousand ; but he must let half of it stick to the Pullwool fingers. The same arrangement was made with Mr. Green and Mr. Sharp and Mr. Bummer and Mr. Pickpurse and Mr. Buncombe. It was a game of snacks, half to you and half to me ; and sometimes it was more than snacks,—a thousand for you two and a thousand for me too.

With such a greasing of the wheels, you may imagine that the machinery of the ring worked to a charm. In the city and in the legislature and throughout the State there was the liveliest buzzing and humming and clicking of political wheels and cranks and cogs that had ever been known in those hitherto pastoral localities. The case of Fastburg against Slowburg was put in a hundred ways, and proved as sure as it was put. It really seemed to the eager burghers as if they already heard the clink of hammers on a new State-House and beheld a perpetual legislature sitting on their fences and curbstones until the edifice should be finished. The great wire-puller and his gang of stipendiaries were the objects of popular gratitude and adoration. The landlord of the hotel which Mr. Pullwool patronized actually would not take pay for that gentleman's board.

" No, sir !" declared this simple Boniface, turning crimson with enthusiasm. " You are going to put thousands of dollars into my purse, and I'll take nothing out of yours. And any little thing in the way of cigars and whiskey that you want, sir, why, call for it. It's my treat, sir."

" Thank you, sir," kindly smiled the great man. " That's what I call the square thing. Mr. Boniface, you are a gentleman and a scholar ; and I'll mention your admirable house to my friends. By the way, I shall have to leave you for a few days."

" Going to leave us !" exclaimed Mr. Boniface, aghast. " I hope not till this job is put through."

" I must run about a bit," muttered Pullwool,

confidentially. "A little turn through the State, you understand, to stir up the country districts. Some of the members ain't as hot as they should be, and I want to set their constituents after them. Nothing like getting on a few deputations."

"Oh, exactly!" chuckled Mr. Boniface, ramming his hands into his pockets and cheerfully jingling a bunch of keys and a penknife for lack of silver. It was strange indeed that he should actually see the Devil in Mr. Pullwool's eye and should not have a suspicion that he was in danger of being humbugged by him. "And your rooms?" he suggested. "How about them?"

"I keep them," replied the lobbyist, grandly, as if blaspheming the expense—to Boniface. "Our friends must have a little hole to meet in. And while you are about it, Mr. Boniface, see that they get something to drink and smoke; and we'll settle it between us."

"Pre—cisely!" laughed the landlord, as much as to say, "My treat!"

And so Mr. Pullwool, that Pericles and Lorenzo de' Medici rolled in one, departed for a season from the city which he ruled and blessed. Did he run about the State and preach and crusade in behalf of Fastburg, and stir up the bucolic populations to stir up their representatives in its favor? Not a bit of it; the place that he went to and the only place that he went to was Slowburg; yes, covering up his tracks in his usual careful style, he made direct for the rival of Fastburg. What did he propose to

do there ? Oh, how can we reveal the whole duplicity
and turpitude of Ananias Pullwool ? The subject
is too vast for a merely human pen ; it requires the
literary ability of a recording angel. Well, we must
get our feeble lever under this boulder of wicked-
ness as we can, and do our faint best to expose all
the reptiles and slimy things beneath it.

The first person whom this apostle of lobbyism
called upon in Slowburg was the mayor of that tot-
tering capital.

" My name is Pullwool," he said to the official,
and he said it with an almost enviable ease of impudence, for he was used to introducing himself
to people who despised and detested him. " I
want to see you confidentially about this capital
ring which is making so much trouble."

" I thought you were in it," replied the mayor,
turning very red in the face, for he had heard of
Mr. Pullwool as the leader of said ring ; and being
an iracund man, he was ready to knock his head
off.

" In it !" exclaimed the possessed one. " I wish
I was. It's a fat thing. More than fifty thousand
dollars paid out already !"

" Good gracious !" exclaimed the mayor in de-
spair.

" By the way, this is between ourselves," added
Pullwool. " You take it so, I hope. Word of
honor, eh ?"

" Why, if you have anything to communicate
that will help us, why, of course, I promise se-

crecy," stammered the mayor. "Yes, certainly ;
word of honor."

"Well, I've been looking about among those
fellows a little," continued Ananias. "I've kept
my eyes and ears open. It's a way I have. And
I've learned a thing or two that it will be to your
advantage to know. Yes, sir ! fifty thousand dollars !—the city has voted it and paid it, and the ring
has got it. That's why they are all working so.
And depend upon it, they'll carry the legislature
and turn Slowburg out to grass, unless you wake
up and do something."

"By heavens !" exclaimed the iracund mayor,
turning red again. "It's a piece of confounded
rascality. It ought to be exposed."

"No, don't expose it," put in Mr. Pullwool,
somewhat alarmed. "That game never works. Of
course they'd deny it and swear you down, for
bribing witnesses is as easy as bribing members.
I'll tell you what to do. Beat them at their own
weapons. Raise a purse that will swamp theirs.
That's the way the world goes. It's an auction.
The highest bidder gets the article."

Well, the result of it all was that the city magnates of Slowburg did just what had been done by
the city magnates of Fastburg, only, instead of
voting fifty thousand dollars into the pockets of the
ring, they voted sixty thousand. With a portion
of this money about him, and with authority to
draw for the rest on proper vouchers, Mr. Pullwool, his tongue in his cheek, bade farewell to

his new allies. As a further proof of the ready wit and solid impudence of this sublime politician and model of American statesmen, let me here introduce a brief anecdote. Leaving Slowburg by the cars, he encountered a gentleman from Fastburg, who saluted him with tokens of amazement, and said, " What are you doing here, Mr. Pullwool ?"

"Oh, just breaking up these fellows a little," whispered the man with the Devil in him. " They were making too strong a fight. I had to *see* some of them," putting one hand behind his back and rubbing his fingers together, to signify that there had been a taking of bribes. " But be shady about it. For the sake of the good cause, keep quiet. Mum's the word."

The reader can imagine how briskly the fight between the two capitals reopened when Mr. Pullwool re-entered the lobby. Slowburg now had its adherents, and they struggled like men who saw money in their warfare, and they struggled not in vain. To cut a very long story very short, to sum the whole of an exciting drama in one sentence, the legislature kicked overboard the bill to make Fastburg the sole seat of government. Nothing had come of the whole row, except that a pair of simple little cities had spent over one hundred thousand dollars, and that the capital ring, fighting on both sides and drawing pay from both sides, had lined its pockets, while the great creator of the ring had crammed his to bursting.

" What does this mean, Mr. Pullwool ?" de-

manded the partially honest and entirely puzzled
Tom Dicker, when he had discovered by an un-
official count of noses how things were going.
"Fastburg has spent all its money for nothing. It
won't be sole capital, after all."

"I never expected it would be," replied Pull.
wool, so tickled by the Devil that was in him that
he could not help laughing. "I never wanted it to
be. Why, it would spoil the little game. This is a
trick that can be played every year."

"Oh!" exclaimed Mr. Dicker, and was dumb
with astonishment for a minute.

"Didn't you see through it before?" grinned the
grand master of all guile and subtlety.

"I did not," confessed Mr. Dicker, with a mixt-
ure of shame and abhorrence. "Well," he presently added, recovering himself, "shall we settle?"

"Oh, certainly, if you are ready," smiled Pullwool, with the air of a man who has something
coming to him.

"And what, exactly, will be my share?" asked
Dicker, humbly.

"What do you mean?" stared Pullwool, apparently in the extremity of amazement.

"You said *snacks*, didn't you?" urged Dicker,
trembling violently.

"Well, *snacks* it is," replied Pullwool. "Haven't
you had a thousand?"

"Yes," admitted Dicker.

"Then you owe me five hundred?"

Mr. Dicker did not faint, though he came very

near it, but he staggered out of the room as white as a sheet, for he was utterly crushed by this diabolical impudence.

That very day Mr. Pullwool left for Washington, and the Devil left for *his* place, each of them sure to find the other when he wanted him, if indeed their roads lay apart.

LOST IN THE FOG.

By Noah Brooks. .

"DOWN with your helm! you'll have us hard and fast aground!"

My acquaintance with Captain Booden was at that time somewhat limited, and if possible I knew less of the difficult and narrow exit from Bolinas Bay than I did of Captain Booden. So with great trepidation I jammed the helm hard down, and the obedient little Lively Polly fell off easily, and we were over the bar and gliding gently along under the steep bluff of the Mesa, whose rocky edge, rising sheer from the beach and crowned with dry grass, rose far above the pennon of the little schooner. I did not intend to deceive Captain Booden, but being anxious to work my way down to San Francisco, I had shipped as "able seaman" on the Lively Polly, though it was a long day since I had handled a foresheet or anything bigger than

the little plungers which hover about Bolinas Bay;
and latterly I had been ranching it at Point Reyes,
so what could I know about the bar and the shoals
of the harbor, I would like to know? We had
glided out of the narrow channel which is skirted
on one side by a long sandspit that curves around
and makes the southern and western shelter of the
bay, and on the other side by a huge elevated tongue
of table-land, called by the inhabitants thereabouts
the Mesa. High, precipitous, perpendicular, level,
and dotted with farm-houses, this singular bit of
land stretches several miles out southward to sea,
bordered with a rocky beach, and tapered off into
the wide ocean with Duxbury Reef—a dangerous
rocky reef, curving down to the southward and
almost always white with foam, save when the sea
is calm, and then the great lazy green waves eddy
noiselessly over the half-hidden rocks, or slip like
oil over the dreadful dangers which they hide.

Behind us was the lovely bay of Bolinas, blue and
sparkling in the summer afternoon sun, its borders
dotted with thrifty ranches, and the woody ravines
and bristling Tamalpais Range rising over all. The
tide was running out, and only a peaceful swash
whispered along the level sandy beach on our left,
where the busy sandpiper chased the playful wave
as it softly rose and fell along the shore. On the
higher centre of the sandspit which shuts in the bay
on that side, a row of ashy-colored gulls sunned
themselves, and blinked at us sleepily as we drifted
slowly out of the channel, our breeze cut off by the

Mesa that hemmed us in on the right. I have told you that I did not much pretend to seamanship, but I was not sorry that I had taken passage on the Lively Polly, for there is always something novel and fascinating to me in coasting a region which I have heretofore known only by its hills, cañons, and sea-beaches. The trip is usually made from Bolinas Bay to San Francisco in five or six hours, when wind and tide favor; and I could bear being knocked about by Captain Booden for that length of time, especially as there was one other hand on board—— "Lanky" he was called—but whether a foremast hand or landsman I do not know. He had been teaching school at Jaybird Cañon, and was a little more awkward with the running rigging of the Lively Polly than I was. Captain Booden was, therefore, the main reliance of the little twenty-ton schooner, and if her deck-load of firewood and cargo of butter and eggs ever reached a market, the skilful and profane skipper should have all the credit thereof.

The wind died away, and the sea, before ruffled with a wholesale breeze, grew as calm as a sheet of billowy glass, heaving only in long, gentle undulations on which the sinking sun bestowed a green and golden glory, dimmed only by the white fog-bank that came drifting slowly up from the Farra-lones, now shut out from view by the lovely haze. Captain Booden gazed morosely on the western horizon, and swore by a big round oath that we should not have a capful of wind if that fog-bank did not lift. But we were fairly out of the bay;

the Mesa was lessening in the distance, and as we
drifted slowly southward the red-roofed buildings
on its level rim grew to look like toy-houses, and
we heard the dull moan of the ebb-tide on Duxbury
Reef on our starboard bow. The sea grew dead
calm and the wind fell quite away, but still we
drifted southward, passing Rocky Point and peering
curiously into Pilot' Boat Cove, which looked so
strangely unfamiliar to me from the sea, though I
had fished in its trout-brooks many a day, and had
hauled driftwood from the rocky beach to Johnson's ranch in times gone by. The tide turned
after sundown, and Captain Booden thought we
ought to get a bit of wind then; but it did not come,
and the fog crept up and up the glassy sea, rolling
in huge wreaths of mist, shutting out the surface of
the water, and finally the gray rocks of North
Heads were hidden, and little by little the shore
was curtained from our view and we were becalmed
in the fog.

To say that the skipper swore would hardly de-
scribe his case. He cursed his luck, his stars, his
foretop, his main hatch, his blasted foolishness, his
lubberly crew—Lanky and I—and a variety of other
persons and things; but all to no avail. Night
came on, and the light on North Heads gleamed at
us with a sickly eye through the deepening fog.
We had a bit of luncheon with us, but no fire, and
were fain to content ourselves with cold meat, bread,
and water, hoping that a warm breakfast in San
Francisco would make some amends for our present

short rations. But the night wore on, and we were still tumbling about in the rising sea without wind enough to fill our sails, a rayless sky overhead, and with breakers continually under our lee. Once we saw lights on shore, and heard the sullen thud of rollers that smote against the rocks; it was aggravating, as the fog lifted for a space, to see the cheerful windows of the Cliff House, and almost hear the merry calls of pleasure-seekers as they muffled themselves in their wraps and drove gayly up the hill, reckless of the poor homeless mariners who were drifting comfortlessly about so near the shore they could not reach. We got out the sweeps and rowed lustily for several hours, steering by the compass and taking our bearings from the cliff.

But we lost our bearings in the maze of currents in which we soon found ourselves, and the dim shore melted away in the thickening fog. To add to our difficulties, Captain Booden put his head most frequently into the cuddy; and when it emerged, he smelt dreadfully of gin. Lanky and I held a secret council, in which we agreed, in case he became intoxicated, we would rise up in mutiny and work the vessel on our own account. He shortly "lost his head," as Lanky phrased it; and slipping down on the deck, went quietly into the sleep of the gin-drunken. At four o'clock in the morning the gray fog grew grayer with the early dawning; and as I gazed with weary eyes into the vague unknown that shut us in, Booden roused him from his booze, and seizing the tiller from my hand, bawled : " 'Bout ship, you swab ! we're on the Farralones !" And sure enough, there loomed right under our starboard quarter a group of con- ical rocks, steeply rising from the restless blue sea. Their wild white sides were crowded with chattering sea-fowl ; and far above, like a faint nimbus in the sky, shone the feeble rays of the lighthouse lantern, now almost quenched by the dull gleam of day that crept up from the water. The helm was jammed hard down. There was no time to get out sweeps ; but still drifting helplessly, we barely grazed the bare rocks of the islet, and swung clear, slinking once more into the gloom.

Our scanty stock of provisions and water was gone ; but there was no danger of starvation, for the generous product of the henneries and dairies of Bolinas filled the vessel's hold—albeit raw eggs and butter without bread might only serve as a barrier against famine. So we drifted and tumbled about—still no wind and no sign of the lifting of the fog. Once in a while it would roll upward and show a long, flat expanse of water, tempting us to believe that the blessed sky was coming out at last ; but soon the veil fell again, and we aimlessly won- dered where we were and whither we were drifting. There is something awful and mysterious in the shadowy nothingness that surrounds one in a fog at sea. You fancy that out of that impenetrable mist may suddenly burst some great disaster or danger. Strange shapes appear to be forming them- selves in the obscurity out of which they emerge, and the eye is wearied beyond expression with looking into a vacuity which continually promises to evolve into something, but never does.

Thus idly drifting, we heard, first, the creaking of a block, then a faint wash of sea; and out of the white depths of the fog came the bulky hull of a full-rigged ship. Her sails were set, but she made scarcely steerage way. Her rusty sides and general look bespoke a long voyage just concluding; and we found on hailing her that she was the British ship Marathon, from Calcutta for San Francisco. We boarded the Marathon, though almost in sight of our own port, with something of the feeling that shipwrecked seamen may have when they reach land. It was odd that we, lost and wandering as we were, should be thus encountered in the vast unknown where we were drifting by a strange ship; and though scarcely two hours' sail from home, should be supplied with bread and water by a Brit- isher from the Indies. We gave them all the infor- mation we had about the pilots, whom we wanted so much to meet ourselves; and after following slowly for a few hours by the huge side of our strange friend, parted company—the black hull and huge spars of the Indiaman gradually lessening in the mist that shut her from our view. We had touched a chord that bound us to our fellow-men but it was drawn from our hands, and the unfath- omable abyss in which we floated had swallowed up each human trace, except what was comprised on the contracted deck of the Lively Polly, where Cap-

tain Booden sat glumly whittling, and Lanky med-
itatively peered after the disappeared Marathon, as
though his soul and all his hopes had gone with her.
The deck, with its load of cord-wood ; the sails and
rigging ; the sliding-hutch of the little cuddy ; and
all the features of the Lively Polly, but yesterday
so unfamiliar, were now as odiously wearisome as
though I had known them for a century. It seemed
as if I had never known any other place.

All that day we floated aimlessly along, moved
only by the sluggish currents, which shifted occa-
sionally, but generally bore us westward and southward ; not a breath of wind arose, and our sails
were as useless as though we had been on dry land.
Night came on again, and found us still entirely
without reckoning and as completely " at sea " as
ever before. To add to our discomfort, a drizzling
rain, unusual for the season of the year, set in, and
we cowered on the wet deck-load, more than ever
disgusted with each other and the world. During
the night a big ocean steamer came plunging and
crashing through the darkness, her lights gleaming
redly through the dense medium as she cautiously
felt her way past us, falling off a few points as she
heard our hail. We lay right in her path, but with
tin horns and a wild Indian yell from the versatile
Lanky managed to make ourselves heard, and the
mysterious stranger disappeared in the fog as suddenly as she had come, and we were once more
alone in the darkness.

The night wore slowly away, and we made out

to catch a few hours' sleep, standing "watch and watch" with each other of our slender crew. Day dawned again, and we broke our fast with the last of the Marathon's biscuit, having "broken cargo" to eke out our cold repast with some of the Bolinas butter and eggs which we were taking to a mòst unexpected market.

Suddenly, about six o'clock in the morning, we heard the sound of breakers ahead, and above the sullen roar of the surf I distinctly heard the tink. lings of a bell. We got out our sweeps and had commenced to row wearily once more, when the fog lifted and before us lay the blessed land. A high range of sparsely wooded hills, crowned with rocky ledges, and with abrupt slopes covered with dry brown grass, running to the water's edge, form-ed the background of the picture. Nearer, a tongue of high land, brushy and rocky, made out from the main shore, and curving southward, formed a shel-ter to what seemed a harbor within. Against the precipitous point the sea broke with a heavy blow, and a few ugly peaks of rock lifted their heads above the heaving green of the sea. High up above the sky-line rose one tall, sharp, blue peak, yet veiled in the floating mist, but its base melted away into a mass of verdure that stretched from the shore far up the mountain-side. Our sweeps were now used to bring us around the point, and cautiously pulling in, we opened a lovely bay bordered with orchards and vineyards, in the midst of which was a neat village, glittering white in the sunshine, and clustered around an old-fashioned mission church, whose quaint gable and tower reminded us of the buildings of the early Spanish settlers of the country. As we neared the shore (there was no landing-place) we could see an unwonted commotion in the clean streets, and a flag was run up to the top of a white staff that stood in the midst of a plaza. Captain Booden returned the compliment by hoisting the Stars and Stripes at our mainmast head, but was sorely bothered with the mingled dyes of the flag on shore. A puff of air blew out its folds, and to our surprise disclosed the Mexican national standard.

. "Blast them greasers," said the patriotic skipper, "if they ain't gone and histed a Mexican cactus flag, then I'm blowed." He seriously thought of hauling down his beloved national colors again, resenting the insult of hoisting a foreign flag on American soil. He pocketed the affront, however, remarking that "they probably knew that a Bolinas butter-boat was not much of a fightist anyway."

We dropped anchor gladly, Captain Booden being wholly at a loss as to our whereabouts. We judged that we were somewhere south of the Golden Gate, but what town this was that slept so tranquilly in the summer sun, and what hills were these that walled in the peaceful scene from the rest of the world, we could not tell. The village seemed awakening from its serene sleepiness, and one by one the windows of the adobe cottages swung open as if the people rubbed their long-closed eyes at some unwonted sight; and the doors gradually opened as though their dumb lips would hail us and ask who were these strangers that vexed the quiet waters of their bay. But two small fishing-boats lay at anchor, and these Booden said reminded him of Christopher Columbus or Noah's Ark, they were so clumsy and antique in build.

We hauled our boat up alongside, and all hands got in and went ashore. As we landed, a little shudder seemed to go through the sleepy old place, as if it had been rudely disturbed from its comfortable nap, and a sudden sob of sea air swept through the quiet streets as though the insensate houses had actually breathed the weary sigh of awaking. The buildings were low and white, with dark-skinned children basking in the doors, and grass hammocks swinging beneath open verandas. There were no stores, no sign of business, and no sound of vehicles or labor; all was as decorous and quiet, to use the skipper's description, "as if the people had slicked up their door-yards, whitewashed their houses, and gone to bed." It was just like a New England Sabbath in a Mexican village.

And this fancy was further colored by a strange procession which now met us as we went up from the narrow beach, having first made fast our boat. A lean Mexican priest, with an enormous shovel hat and particularly shabby cassock, came toward us, followed by a motley crowd of Mexicans, prominent among whom was a pompous old man clad in a seedy Mexican uniform and wearing a trailing rapier at his side. The rest of the procession was brought up with a crowd of shy women, dark-eyed and tawny and all poorly clad, though otherwise comfortable enough in condition. These hung back and wonderingly looked at the strange faces, as though they had never seen the like before. The old padre lifted his skinny hands, and said something in Spanish which I did not understand.

"Why, the old mummy is slinging his popish blessings at us!" This was Lanky's interpretation of the kindly priest's paternal salutation. And, sure enough, he was welcoming us to the shore of San Ildefonso with holy fervor and religious phrase.

"I say," said Booden, a little testily, "what did you say was the name of this place, and where away does it lay from 'Frisco?" In very choice Castilian, as Lanky declared, the priest rejoined that he did not understand the language in which Booden was speaking. "Then bring on somebody that does," rejoined that irreverent mariner, when due interpretation had been made. The padre protested that no one in the village understood the English tongue. The skipper gave a long low whistle of suppressed astonishment, and wondered if we had drifted down to Lower California in two days and nights, and had struck a Mexican settlement. The colors on the flagstaff and the absence of any Americans gave some show of reason to this startling conclusion; and Lanky, who was now the interpreter of the party, asked the name of the place, and was again told that it was San Ildefonso; but when he asked what country it was in and how far it was to San Francisco, he was met with a polite "I do not understand you, Señor." Here was a puzzle : becalmed in a strange port only two days drift from the city of San Francisco; a town which the schoolmaster declared was not laid down on any map; a population that spoke only Spanish and did not know English when they heard it; a Mexican flag flying over the town, and an educated priest who did not know what we meant when we asked how far it was to San Francisco. Were we bewitched?

Accepting a hospitable invitation from the padre, we sauntered up to the plaza, where we were ushered into a long, low room, which might once have been a military barrack-room. It was neatly whitewashed and had a hard clay floor, and along the walls were a few ancient firelocks and a venerable picture of "His Excellency, General Santa Aña, President of the Republic of Mexico," as a legend beneath it set forth. Breakfast of chickens, vegetables, bread, and an excellent sort of country wine (this last being served in a big earthen bottle) was served up to us on the long unpainted table that stood in the middle of the room. During the repast our host, the priest, sat with folded hands intently regarding us, while the rest of the people clustered around the door and open windows, eying us with indescribable and incomprehensible curiosity. If we had been visitors from the moon we could not have attracted more attention. Even the stolid Indians, a few of whom strolled lazily

about, came and gazed at us until the pompous old
man in faded Mexican uniform drove them noisily
away from the window, where they shut out the
light and the pleasant morning air, perfumed with
heliotropes, verbenas, and sweet herbs that grew
luxuriantly about the houses.

The padre had restrained his curiosity out of rigid
politeness until we had eaten, when he began by
asking, "Did our galleon come from Manila?"
We told him that we only came from Bolinas;
whereat he said once more, with a puzzled look of
pain, "I do not understand you, Señor." Then
pointing through the open doorway to where the
Lively Polly peacefully floated at anchor, he asked
what ensign was that which floated at her masthead.
Lanky proudly, but with some astonishment, replied: "That's the American flag, Señor." At this
the seedy old man in uniform eagerly said: "Americanos! Americanos! why, I saw some of those people and that flag at Monterey." Lanky asked him
if Monterey was not full of Americans, and did not
have plenty of flags. The Ancient replied that he
did not know; it was a long time since he had been
there. Lanky observed that perhaps he had never
been there. "I was there in 1835," said the Ancient.
This curious speech being interpreted to Captain
Booden, that worthy remarked that he did not believe that he had seen a white man since.

After an ineffectual effort to explain to the company where Bolinas was, we rose and went out for
a view of the town. It was beautifully situated on

a gentle rise which swelled up from the water's edge and fell rapidly off in the rear of the town into a deep ravine, where a brawling mountain stream supplied a little flouring-mill with motive power. Beyond the ravine were small fields of grain, beans and lentils on the rolling slopes, and back of these rose the dark, dense vegetation of low hills, while over all were the rough and ragged ridges of mountains closing in all the scene. The town itself, as I have said, was white and clean; the houses were low-browed, with windows secured by wooden shutters, only a few glazed sashes being seen anywhere. Out of these openings in the thick adobe walls of the humble homes of the villagers flashed the curious, the abashed glances of many a dark-eyed senorita, who fled, laughing, as we approached. The old church was on the plaza, and in its odd-shaped turret tinkled the little bell whose notes had sounded the morning angelus when we were knocking about in the fog outside. High up on its quaintly arched gable was inscribed in antique letters "1796." In reply to a sceptical remark from Lanky, Booden declared that "the old shell looked as though it might have been built in the time of Ferdinand and Isabella, for that matter." The worthy skipper had a misty idea that all old Spanish buildings were built in the days of these famous sovereigns.

Hearing the names of Ferdinand and Isabella, the padre gravely and reverentially asked: "And is the health of His Excellency, General Santa Aña, whom God protect, still continued to him?"

With great amazement, Lanky replied: "Santa Aña! why, the last heard of him was that he was keeping a cockpit in Havana; some of the newspapers published an obituary of him about six months ago, but I believe he is alive yet somewhere."

A little flush of indignation mantled the old man's cheek, and with a tinge of severity in his voice he said: "I have heard that shameful scandal about our noble President once before, but you must excuse me if I ask you not to repeat it. It is true he took away our Pious Fund some years since, but he is still our revered President, and I would not hear him ill-spoken of any more than our puissant and mighty Ferdinand, of whom you just spoke—may he rest in glory!" and here the good priest crossed himself devoutly.

"What is the old priest jabbering about?" asked Captain Booden, impatiently; for he was in haste to "get his bearings" and be off. When Lanky replied, he burst out: "Tell him that Santa Aña is not President of Mexico any more than I am, and that he hasn't amounted to a row of pins since California was part of the United States."

Lanky faithfully interpreted this fling at the ex-President, whereupon the padre, motioning to the Ancient to put up his rapier, which had leaped out of its rusty scabbard, said: "Nay, Señor, you would insult an old man. We have never been told yet by our government that the Province of California was alienated from the great Republic of Mexico, and we owe allegiance to none save the nation whose flag we love so well;" and the old man turned his tear-dimmed eyes toward the ragged standard of Mexico that drooped from the staff in the plaza. Continuing, he said: "Our noble country has strangely forgotten us, and though we watch the harbor-entrance year after year, no tidings ever comes. The galleon that was to bring us stores has never been seen on the horizon yet, and we seem lost in the fog."

The schoolmaster of Jaybird Cañon managed to tell us what the priest had said, and then asked when he had last heard of the outside world. "It was in 1837," said he, sadly, "when we sent a courier to the Mission del Carmelo, at Monterey, for tidings from New Spain. He never came back, and the great earthquake which shook the country hereabout opened a huge chasm across the country just back of the Sierra yonder, and none dared to cross over to the main land. The saints have defended us in peace, and it is the will of Heaven that we shall stay here by ourselves until the Holy Virgin, in answer to our prayers, shall send us deliverance."

Here was a new revelation. This was an old Spanish Catholic mission, settled in 1796, called San Ildefonso, which had evidently been overlooked for nearly forty years, and had quietly slept in an unknown solitude while the country had been transferred to the United States from the flag that still idly waved over it. Lost in the fog! Here was a whole town lost in a fog of years. Empires

and dynasties had risen and fallen ; the world had
repeatedly been shaken to its centre, and this people had heeded it not ; a great civil war had ravaged
the country to which they now belonged, and they
knew not of it ; poor Mexico herself had been torn
with dissensions and had been insulted with an em-
pire, and these peaceful and weary watchers for
tidings from " New Spain" had recked nothing of
all these things. All around them the busy State of
California was scarred with the eager pick of gold-
seekers or the shining share of the husbandman ;
towns and cities had sprung up where these patri-
archs had only known of vast cattle ranges or
sleepy missions of the Roman Catholic Fathers.
They knew nothing of the great city of San Francisco, with its busy marts and crowded harbor ; and
thought of its broad bay—if they thought of it at
all—as the lovely shore of Yerba Buena, bounded
by bleak hills and almost unvexed by any keel.
The political storms of forty years had gone hurt-
less over their heads, and in a certain sort of dream-
less sleep San Ildefonso had still remained true to
the red, white, and green flag that had long since
disappeared from every part of the State save here,
where it was still loved and revered as the banner
of the soil.

The social and political framework of the town had
been kept up through all these years. There had been
no connection with the fountain of political power,
but the town was ruled by the legally elected
Ayuntamiento, or Common Council, of which the

Ancient, Señor Apolonario Maldonado, was President or Alcade. They were daily looking for advices from Don José Castro, Governor of the loyal province of California; and so they had been looking daily for forty years. We asked if they had not heard from any of the prying Yankees who crowd the country. Father Ignacio—for that was the padre's name—replied: "Yes; five years ago, when the winter rains had just set in, a tall, spare man, who talked some French and some Spanish, came down over the mountains with a pack containing pocket-knives, razors, soap, perfumery, laces, and other curious wares, and besought our people to purchase. We have not much coin, but were disposed to treat him Christianly, until he did declare that President General Santa Aña, whom may the saints defend! was a thief and gambler, and had gambled away the Province of California to the United States; whereupon we drave him hence, the Ayuntamiento sending a trusty guard to see him two leagues from the borders of the Pueblo. But months after, we discovered his pack and such of his poor bones as the wild beasts of prey had not carried off, at the base of a precipice where he had fallen. His few remains and his goods were together buried on the mountain-side, and I lamented that we had been so hard with him. But the saints forbid that he should go back and tell where the people of San Ildefonso were waiting to hear from their own neglectful country, which may Heaven defend, bless, and prosper."

The little town took on a new interest to us cold
outsiders after hearing its strange and almost im-
probable story. We could have scarcely believed
that San Ildefonso had actually been overlooked in
the transfer of the country from Mexico to the
United States, and had for nearly forty years been
hidden away between the Sierra and the sea; but
if we were disposed to doubt the word of the good
father, here was intrinsic evidence of the truth of
his narrative. There were no Americans here:
only the remnants of the old Mexican occupation
and the civilized Indians. No traces of later civilization could be found; but the simple dresses,
tools, implements of husbandry, and household
utensils were such as I have seen in the half-civil-
ized wilds of Central America. The old mill in the
cañon behind the town was a curiosity of clumsi-
ness, and nine-tenths of the water-power of the ar-
roya that supplied it were wasted. Besides, until
now, who ever heard of such a town in California
as San Ildefonso? Upon what map can any such
headland and bay be traced? and where are the his-
toric records of the pueblo whose well-defined
boundaries lay palpably before us? I have dwelt
upon this point, about which I naturally have some
feeling, because of the sceptical criticism which my
narrative has since provoked. There are some people in the world who never will believe anything
that they have not seen, touched, or tasted for themselves; California has her share of such.

Captain Booden was disposed to reject Father

Ignacio's story, until I called his attention to the fact that this was a tolerable harbor for small craft, and yet had never before been heard of ; that he never knew of such a town, and that if any of his numerous associates in the marine profession knew of the town or harbor of San Ildefonso, he surely would have heard of it from them. He restrained his impatience to be off long enough to allow Father Ignacio to gather from us a few chapters of the world's history for forty years past. The discovery of gold in California, the settlement of the country and the Pacific Railroad were not so much account to him, somehow, as the condition of Europe, the Church of Mexico, and what had become of the Pious Fund ; this last I discovered had been a worrisome subject to the good Father. I did not know what it was myself, but I believe it was the alienation from the church of certain moneys and incomes which were transferred to speculators by the Mexican Congress, years and years ago.

I was glad to find that we were more readily believed by Father Ignacio and the old Don than our Yankee predecessor had been ; perhaps we were believed more on his corroborative evidence. The priest, however, politely declined to believe all we said—that was evident ; and the Don steadily refused to believe that California had been transferred to the United States. It was a little touching to see Father Ignacio's doubt and hopes struggle in his withered face as he heard in a few brief sentences the history of his beloved land and Church

for forty years past. His eye kindled or it was be-
dewed with tears as he listened, and an occasional
flash of resentment flushed his cheek when he heard
something that shook his ancient faith in the estab-
lished order of things. To a proposition to take a
passage with us to San Francisco, he replied warmly
that he would on no account leave his flock, nor
attempt to thwart the manifest will of Heaven that
the town should remain unheard of until delivered
from its long sleep by the same agencies that had
cut it off from the rest of the world. Neither would
he allow any of the people to come with us.

And so we parted. We went out with the turn
of the tide, Father Ignacio and the Ancient accompanying us to the beach, followed by a crowd of the
townsfolk, who carried for us water and provisions
for a longer voyage than ours promised to be.
The venerable priest raised his hands in parting
blessing as we shoved off, and I saw two big tears
roll down the furrowed face of Señor Maldonado,
who looked after us as a stalwart old warrior might
look at the departure of a band of hopeful comrades
leaving him to fret in monkish solitude while they
were off to the wars again. Wind and tide served,
and in a few minutes the Lively Polly rounded the
point, and looking back, I saw the yellow haze of
the afternoon sun sifted sleepily over all the place;
the knots of white-clad people standing statuesque
and motionless as they gazed; the flag of Mexico
faintly waving in the air; and with a sigh of relief
a slumbrous veil seemed to fall over all the scene:

and as our boat met the roll of the current outside the headland, the gray rocks of the point shut out the fading view, and we saw the last of San Ildefonso.

Captain Booden had gathered enough from the people to know that we were somewhere south of San Francisco (the Lively Polly had no chart or nautical instruments on board of course), and so he determined to coast cautiously along northward, marking the shore line in order to be able to guide other navigators to the harbor. But a light mist crept down the coast, shutting out the view of the headlands, and by midnight we had stretched out to sea again, and we were once more out of our reckoning. At daybreak, however, the fog lifted, and we found ourselves in sight of land, and a brisk breeze blowing, we soon made Pigeon Point, and before noon were inside the Golden Gate, and ended our long and adventurous cruise from Bolinas Bay by hauling into the wharf of San Francisco.

I have little left to tell. Of the shameful way in which our report was received, every newspaper reader knows. At first there were some persons, men of science and reading, who were disposed to believe what we said. I printed in one of the daily newspapers an account of what we had discovered, giving a full history of San Ildefonso as Father Ignacio had given it to us. Of course, as I find is usual in such cases, the other newspapers pooh-poohed the story their contemporary had published to their exclusion, and made themselves very merry over what they were pleased to term " The Great San Ildefonso Sell." I prevailed on Captain Booden to make a short voyage down the coast in search of the lost port. But we never saw the headland, the ridge beyond the town, nor anything that looked like these landmarks, though we went down as far as San Pedro Bay and back twice or three times. It actually did seem that the whole locality had been swallowed up, or had vanished into air. In vain did I bring the matter to the notice of the merchants and scientific men of San Francisco. Nobody would fit out an exploring expedition by land or sea ; those who listened at first finally inquired "if there was any money in it ?" I could not give an affirmative answer, and they turned away with the discouraging remark that the California Academy of Natural Science and the Society of Pioneers were the only bodies interested in the fate of our lost city. Even Captain Booden somehow lost all interest in the enterprise, and returned to his Bolinas coasting with the most stolid indifference. I combated the attacks of the newspapers with facts and depositions of my fellow-voyagers as long as I could, until one day the editor of the Daily Trumpeter (I suppress the real name of the sheet) coldly told me that the public were tired of the story of San Ildefonso. It was plain that his mind had been soured by the sarcasms of his contemporaries, and he no longer believed in me.

The newspaper controversy died away and was forgotten, but I have never relinquished the hope of proving the verity of my statements. At one time I expected to establish the truth, having heard that one Zedekiah Murch had known a Yankee peddler who had gone over the mountains of Santa Cruz and never was heard of more. But Zedekiah's memory was feeble, and he only knew that such a story prevailed long ago; so that clue was soon lost again, and the little fire of enthusiasm which it had kindled among a few persons died out. I have not yet lost all hope; and when I think of the regretful conviction that will force itself upon the mind of good Father Ignacio, that we were, after all, impostors, I cannot bear to reflect that I may die and visit the lost town of San Ildefonso no more.